Potent Natural Medicines

MOTHER NATURE'S PHARMACY

J. S. Kidd and Renee A. Kidd

CHELSEA HOUSE
PUBLISHERS
An imprint of Infobase Publishing

This one is for Elliana

◆

Potent Natural Medicines: Mother Nature's Pharmacy

Copyright © 2006, 1998 by J. S. Kidd and Renee A. Kidd

This is a revised edition of Mother Nature's Pharmacy: Potent Plant Medicines
Copyright © 1998 by J. S. Kidd and Renee A. Kidd

Chelsea House
An imprint of Infobase Publishing
132 West 31st Street
New York NY 10001

ISBN-10: 0-8160-5607-2
ISBN-13: 978-0-8160-5607-1

Library of Congress Cataloging-in-Publication Data
Kidd, J. S. (Jerry S.)
    Potent natural medicines : Mother Nature's pharmacy / J. S. Kidd and Renee A. Kidd.
        p. cm.—(Science and society)
    Rev. ed. of Mother Nature's pharmacy.
Includes bibliographical references and index.
ISBN 0-8160-5607-2
    1. Pharmacognosy—Juvenile literature. I. Kidd, Renee A. II. Kidd, J. S. (Jerry S.)
Mother Nature's pharmacy. III. Title. IV. Science and society (Facts On File, Inc.)

RS164.K53 2005
615'.321—dc22   2005041741

Text design by James Scotto-Lavino
Cover design by Pehrsson Design
Illustrations by Sholto Ainslie

Printed in the United States of America

MP FOF 10 9 8 7 6 5 4 3 2

This book is printed on acid-free paper.

Contents

Preface

The products of science and technology influence the lives of all citizens, including young adults. New means of communication and transportation, new ways of doing work and pursuing recreation, new foods and new medicines arrive almost daily. Science also engenders new ways of looking at the world and at other citizens. Likewise, science can raise concerns about moral and ethical values.

Dealing with all such changes requires some resiliency. The needed adaptations by individuals are fostered by knowledge of the inner workings of science and technology and of the researchers and engineers who do the studies and design the products. Consequently, one of the goals of the Science and Society set of books is to illuminate these subjects in a way that is both accurate and understandable.

One of the obstacles in reaching that goal is the fact that almost all the connections between citizens and scientists are impersonal. For example, the direction of study in a specialized field of science is now mainly determined by negotiations between the leaders of research projects and government officials. National elections rarely hinge on questions of science and technology. Such matters are usually relegated to secondary political status. In any case, most of the officials who are concerned with science are not elected but are appointed and are members of large government bureaucracies.

Other influences on the directions taken by science and technology come from other bureaucratic organizations, such as international political bodies, large commercial firms, academic institutions, or philanthropic foundations. However, in recent years, influence has also come from more informal voluntary groups of citizens and citizen action organizations. The scope of the set has been revised to reflect the growing importance of such channels linking citizens to the leaders in science.

The books describe some of the dramatic adventures on the part of the people who do scientific work, show the human side of science, and convey the idea that scientists experience the same kinds of day-to-day frustrations that afflict everyone.

The revisions attempt to show some of the developing trends in the impact of science on sections of the citizenry such as groupings by age or gender—or geographic location. An example is the change in the living conditions in small, rural communities that have come about as a consequence of agricultural mechanization. Finally, the books describe some of the significant strides in the actual findings of science in recent years. Some fields of science such as genetics and molecular biology have gone through a virtual revolution. These radical changes are ongoing. Likewise, the development of natural medicines was recently given social prominence by the establishment of government agencies devoted explicitly to the support of such research.

Science and Society shows the extent to which individuals can have a stake in the enterprise called science and technology—how they can cope with the societal changes entailed and how they can exert some personal influence on what is happening.

Acknowledgments

We thank the administrators, faculty, and staff of the College of Information Studies of the University of Maryland, College Park. In particular, Dean Emeritus Ann Prentice and Associate Dean Diane Barlow at College Park were extraordinarily patient and supportive.

We are also grateful for support and guidance from colleagues at the National Academy of Sciences/ National Research Council in Washington, D.C. Again, special thanks to Anne Mavor and Alexandria Wigdor for their kindly dispositions and to Susan McCutchen for her high spirits.

We appreciate the kindness of Rebecca McGinnis in helping us with our discussion of traditional Chinese medicine.

Lastly, the late Professor Richard Evans Schultes gave us a gentle nudge in the right direction at the right time.

Introduction

Medicine from natural sources has recently become a more prominent concern for the average citizen. One factor behind the increased attention is the need to find new drugs to fight scourges such as HIV/AIDS and severe acute respiratory syndrome (SARS). Similarly, some of the standard antibiotics have become much less effective because microbes have developed drug resistances. New drugs must be developed to take the place of those whose effectiveness has diminished. Meanwhile, drug development has become increasingly expensive and time-consuming, while inventive ideas for new drugs are rare.

Another factor driving citizen concern is the rising cost of medical treatment. For some people these costs lead to a search for nonconventional procedures. For others, the high costs of conventional drugs leads to self-medication with lower-priced products. Based in part on the acceptability of the use of vitamin supplements to remedy subpar feelings, other health-related products, such as herbal materials, have gained popularity. Thus, a wide range of practices such as self-medication and the adoption of treatments outside of conventional medicine have increased in the early years of the 21st century. Medical educators, writing in professional medical literature, have warned practicing physicians to be aware that their patients might be using materials or subjecting themselves to treatments that do not fit in well with standard health-care procedures. In some instances, patients may be taking prescribed medicines at the same time they are consuming other products such as herbal materials. Since medicines can interact in the body, such practices can cause problems.

The rewards for the development of a new drug from natural raw materials can be generous. Consequently, the efforts of explorers and natural products researchers have taken on greater scope and urgency. The rush to find new sources of drugs can mean that the rights of native peoples are sometimes disregarded—even by well-intentioned research scientists. Problems also arise with regard to the ways in which the rewards of a successful drug development are divided. Likewise, many scientists are concerned that tropical forests and other ecological communities may be adversely disturbed by the search for drug-bearing plants and animals.

In the original edition of this book, central topics included the adventures of the plant hunters and the medical consequences of their efforts. The adventure narratives remain and have been expanded. However, more attention is given to the commercial backing of botanical expeditions and the interactions of commercial plant hunters with local native populations. The scope has also been expanded to include animal sources (mainly, insects and sea creatures).

Some attention was also given to the practices of the U.S. government that are intended to regulate the sale and use of natural products. More scope is given to product monitoring and the government's efforts to protect consumers. Such protection means more than just ensuring product safety. Included is the determination that advertising claims are accurate. If misstatements or fraud are found, various governmental agencies are empowered to prosecute the offenders.

A new role for the biomedical research organizations of the government is to bring science to bear on the full range of complementary and alternative health-care procedures. One of the goals is to integrate effective treatments into the range of options available to health-care providers and their patients.

Finally, more of the scientific foundations of drug discovery are explored. Many scientific procedures have changed in the years since the original version was published. For researchers, the most important changes have been in the methods used to evaluate prospective drugs for safety and effectiveness. While in the recent past a laboratory in a major pharmaceutical company might evaluate several hundred candidate compounds in a year, they are now able to process thousands of samples. Innovations in miniaturization of the laboratory tools and major changes in the use of computers and robotics have made a big difference in the cost and speed of the work.

1

Progress in Health Care

Long before historic times, humans used natural products as medicines. In all likelihood, the use of plants for medicinal purposes grew out of the search for plants that were good to eat. This quest might explain the use of garlic as a medicine. Anyone who has ever attempted to eat raw garlic remembers its strong taste and smell. Ancient cooks, too, might have noted that it was not a pleasing food when eaten by itself. Eventually, they realized that the plant was flavorful when cooked with other ingredients. Early medicine men and women, however, may not have regarded garlic as a possible food. These healers reasoned that raw garlic's strong smell might make it a powerful medicine against illness. Even today, some people consider garlic a medicine that helps relieve various health problems.

For more than 50,000 years, humans have experimented with eating many things—both plant and animal. If the experiment revealed a bad-tasting, sickening, or deadly substance, the information was passed from one generation to the next. In the same way, knowledge about substances that helped or cured sick people was communicated to others. Treatments using folk remedies were passed on to successive generations long before the invention of written records.

In some human societies, the results of successful medical treatments were not widely shared. Instead, secrecy was prevalent. Shamans were often considered to have special gifts or

1

powers. Some groups believed only those with these special spiritual connections could have certain knowledge. Because of this shamans sometimes maintained a monopoly on information about medicinal products. Because of their knowledge, they enjoyed a privileged position within their group. Although most shamans were well-intentioned, some took unfair advantage of those who were ill, refusing to use their learning unless they received favors from patients or the families of the sick.

Today, such knowledge is no longer kept secret. The ethics of science requires that accounts of all scientific investigations must indicate the research methods, materials, findings, and conclusions. Therefore, anyone can duplicate the work and arrive at the same result. When applying for a patent, the situation is similar. The inventor must reveal the procedures necessary to accomplish the invention. The inventor's rights are protected by the patent, but the details of the assembly of the device or the steps in a process are made public.

Early Medical Practices

For thousands of years, most medical treatments relied on the use of plants. The ancient founders of science-based medicine were herbalists—people who studied and used plants—who recorded their knowledge in scrolls and books. Greek pioneers such as Hippocrates (ca. 460–ca. 377 B.C.) and Galen (A.D. 129–ca. 199) combined the skills of botanist and pharmacist with those of diagnostician and physician.

In general, ancient physicians were gentle when caring for the sick. They kept the patient warm and dry, and often treated him or her with medicines made from plants. One version of the Hippocratic oath, still recited by newly licensed medical practitioners, contains the phrase, "above all, do no harm." However, during the Middle Ages (period in Europe from

Alchemists and apothecaries were principal sources of medicines in the Middle Ages. (Courtesy of the Photographic Archive Services, National Library of Medicine)

ca. 500 to 1500), the European approach to medical treatment changed and many physicians adopted a "heroic" response to disease. These treatments were often far more intrusive and painful.

To some extent, heroic methods were based on the ancient theory of humors. This theory was advanced in the time before the Christian era and was still in vogue in the early 1500s. According to this theory, the human body contains four key fluids, or humors, which must be kept in balance to maintain good health. The humors were blood, phlegm, black bile, and yellow bile. A personality trait was associated with each of the humors. Someone who was relatively cheerful and active was designated as sanguine. Sanguine people were thought to have a surplus of blood. In contrast, a phlegmatic person was depressed and sluggish. These conditions indicated an excess of phlegm. People now know that these notions about humors are not true.

However, to the practitioners of times past, these ideas provided direction for diagnosis and treatment. For example, if someone became overly active and agitated during an illness, the person was diagnosed as sanguine. Since this indicated too much blood, bloodsucking leeches were placed on the patient's body to remove some of the blood. Other treatments to bring the humors into balance included induced vomiting—by mechanical or chemical means—and deep irrigation of the large bowel. These heroic responses were unpleasant, unsanitary, and often fatal.

The belladonna plant is a source of atropine, a substance used by ophthalmologists to dilate the eye. Native Americans used a tea made from the pulverized roots as a purgative. (Courtesy of Monica S. and Timothy B. Guenther)

Other tactics to cure sickness were based on restoring a balance between the conditions of temperature and dampness. To relieve various ills, patients were sometimes wrapped in very cold, wet cloths and sometimes in hot, dry ones. This method was uncomfortable—but much less injurious than those used to keep the four humors in balance. The health benefits thought to come from steam baths and saunas may have been derived from this theory.

Other heroic treatments were developed during the 19th century. After electricity became available, some patients were treated with electroshock to various parts of the body. The location of the shock depended on the disease and was intended to improve the physical or mental health of the sick person. Other patients were forced to ingest disagreeable substances. In those days, some caregivers reasoned that a painful or disgusting treatment would force the patient to recover to avoid further treatment.

Reforms

In most cases, treatments based on physical abuse were not effective. Consequently, compassionate physicians sought alternative treatments. In the 1780s, William Withering, a Scottish physician, noticed that country folk in England made a herbal tea from the leaves of the foxglove plant. The tea was given as a treatment to those who suffered from abnormal swellings and heart pains. Withering decided to study the use of foxglove leaves as a medicinal substance. His experiments proved that foxglove did help heart conditions, and Withering developed the heart medicine now known as digitalis.

To study the properties of his new medicine, Withering tested digitalis on 163 patients with heart disease. He was one of the first doctors to undertake a systematic evaluation of a therapeutic substance.

Humane physicians used other means to oppose cruel heroic methods. In the 1790s, Samuel Hahnemann, a respected teacher of medicine, advocated bed rest and nourishing food to cure illness. He believed that the human body had extensive powers of recovery and should be allowed to heal itself whenever it could.

Some farsighted individuals investigated methods to prevent people from becoming ill. In the mid-1700s, Lady Mary

Montagu, an English poet, toured the eastern Mediterranean. She returned to England with news of a new technique to protect humanity from smallpox—a very contagious, dangerous, and disfiguring disease. While traveling in Turkey, Lady Montagu learned about the technique of inoculation from local Muslim physicians. Their method was to give the patient a mild form of the disease and hope that the person could recover. Once cured, the patient would never be reinfected with the disease. However, this method was dangerous. Some of those inoculated developed a full-fledged case of smallpox and died. The technique of inoculation needed to be perfected before it could be used safely.

The foxglove plant is the source of digitalis—an effective treatment for congestive heart disease. The active substance was discovered by studying folk medicine practices.
(Courtesy of the Photographic Archive Services, National Library of Medicine)

In the last quarter of the 18th century, William Jenner, an English country doctor, discovered a safe method to inoculate people against smallpox. Jenner had many dairy workers among his patients. Over the years, he observed that cowpox, a common disease among cattle, had some interesting properties. Jenner noted that dairy workers did not became very ill when they caught cowpox from their cows. After they recovered from cowpox, the same workers rarely caught smallpox. The physicians reasoned that a case of cowpox somehow protected the person against smallpox. Around 1780, he injected healthy people with a serum containing a substance taken from the sores of sick cows. The patients developed cowpox but later proved to be immune to smallpox. Although no one—including Jenner—understood why this technique was effective, it became widely used. Over the years, Jenner's discovery saved thousands upon thousands of lives.

Lifestyles

In the United States during the 1830s, several charismatic leaders promoted an unusual idea of disease prevention. Each promised that a radical change in lifestyle would result in a long, disease-free lifetime. Sylvester Graham, the most popular—and one of the most extreme—of these leaders, was a traveling preacher. Graham laid down specific rules to attain good health. He advocated that all his followers adhere to a vegetarian diet that included a nourishing whole-grain biscuit that he had devised—the graham cracker. In addition, his rules included drastic restrictions on the relationship between men and women. When Graham died at the relatively young age of 57, his bold system of life reform met with some skepticism. However, other more realistic reformers followed Graham. Moderation was the approach advocated by leaders such as W. K. Kellogg in the early 1900s.

William Jenner grasped the idea that immunity from a particular disease could develop when the patient survived an infection of that disease. He did so without knowing the cause of the infection. (Courtesy of the Photographic Archive Services, National Library of Medicine)

The Application of Science

By the mid-1800s, advances of a more scientific nature—especially in the field of biology—led to a better understanding of disease. In 1858, the German biologist Rudolph Virchow used a microscope to demonstrate that the progress of a disease could be observed in the affected cells. During the 1850s and 1860s, the French scientist Louis Pasteur showed that microorganisms—organisms that can be observed only under a microscope—were responsible for many diseases. His research proved that a specific disease was caused by a specific microorganism. Pasteur reasoned that if the disease-causing microbe could be killed, the disease would be cured.

Louis Pasteur discovered that microscopic creatures could cause disease. (Courtesy of the Photographic Archive Services, National Library of Medicine)

The German scientist Robert Koch also pursued the idea that a particular microbe was the cause of a particular disease. In 1882, he determined the identity of the tuberculosis microbe that attacks the cells of the lungs. In 1883, he identified the cholera microbe that attacks the cells in the digestive system. These discoveries motivated chemists such as the German bacteriologist Paul Ehrlich to spend a lifetime searching for specific remedies. Around 1900, after many false starts, Ehrlich formulated a compound of arsenic called Salvarsan 606. This medicine was lethal to the microbe that causes syphilis—

a dangerous, sexually trans-mitted disease that attacks cells in the nervous system.

Although new medicines and techniques were in limit-ed use by the turn of the century, doctors, government officials, educators, and the public were dissatisfied with the available medical care. By that time, most people realized that neither lifestyle reforms nor heroic techniques were producing good results. Many poorly informed physi-cians still resorted to painful treatments. In the early 1900s, partly in response to the gen-eral dissatisfaction, a new, sci-entific approach to health care became popular. This approach gained increasing acceptance after scientists

Paul Ehrlich was noted for his persistence. He tried hundreds of compounds before discovering an effective treatment for syphilis. (Courtesy of the Photographic Archive Services, National Library of Medicine)

achieved control over yellow fever, botulism, and other dead-ly diseases. These and other important discoveries radically changed the practice of medicine in industrialized countries.

Science and Medical Education

Medical schools were the first institutions to make major changes. Before 1900, much of medical training was an apprentice system in which physicians allowed students to observe and copy their procedures. After 1910, medical schools in the United States required course work in the basic sciences in addition to clinical observation. Soon, the whole concept of medical education began to change. At first, medical students were required to complete three years of premedical college work. As medicine became a more prestigious profession and the number of applicants increased, medical school administrators sought to reduce the number of would-be physicians. They increased the required period of undergraduate study to four years. These years laid a solid foundation in chemistry and biology in addition to courses in physics and mathematics.

After students were admitted to medical school, the first two years were spent in advanced science training. This training included courses in physiology, human anatomy, and other areas that are necessary to understand the human body. The last two years focused on an extensive study of specific diseases.

In the early days of medical education reform, aspiring doctors rarely saw patients for diagnosis or treatment. In many cases, seven years of preliminary study were required before a young doctor had much contact with a patient. In more recent times, starting in the 1970s, health-care managers complained that new doctors were qualified scientists but knew little about the real needs of patients. Gradually over the past 25 years, many medical schools have begun to involve students with patients throughout their years of medical education prior to their internship experiences.

Today, other changes are being introduced in medical education. For many years, most medical students became general practitioners after graduation. These men and women took care of all medical needs, including delivering babies, setting bones, and curing diseases. By the 1950s, physicians began to specialize in one area, such as heart disease or intestinal problems. At present, U.S. government funding for medical education and health care is supporting the reduction of narrow specialization. Government officials believe that doctors associated with general or family practices can provide better basic health care.

The early 20th-century reforms have had many consequences. The long years of medical training and the high cost of medical education has led to a gradual increase in the income and social status of physicians. The required courses in science have assured better educated and more competent doctors. The reforms also helped to make the profession more effective and efficient. Many dreaded infectious diseases—such as scarlet fever, mumps, and whooping cough—have become far less of a health hazard. New techniques and medicines have reduced deaths due to diseases such as AIDS and cancer. Vaccines and other protective measures have helped to control communicable diseases such as influenza and measles. Today, computers link doctors and other health-care providers so that they can obtain worldwide medical information on patients, medicines, and procedures.

The Expansion of Medical Science

In the 21st century, medical research is being performed in a large number of varied settings. For example, some research is carried out by individual health-care providers who make careful records of the progress of patients undergoing treatment. In accord with a long-standing tradition in the medical community, reports of the outcome of cases are published in the professional literature as a way of sharing down-to-earth, practical experiences among medical colleagues. However, most biomedical research is now conducted by teams of scientists in the setting of large organizations.

One category of medical research organization is the governmental laboratory. Such research facilities have most often grown out of the work on disease prevention in the framework of public health institutions. For example, the U.S. Public Health

Service houses the National Institutes of Health—possibly the largest medical research organization in the world.

A second organizational category is composed of medical schools. Ever since the reforms in medical education that emphasized basic science in the curriculum, medical schools have been a major source of medical research. Most medical schools also function in the setting of a parent university. These universities contain academic departments that are dedicated to basic research fields, such as biology, chemistry and the other disciplines that are relevant to medical progress. Both the medical school faculties and the basic science faculties undertake projects that are paid for in part by tax money. Among the projects are some that foster drug development.

The third organizational category is the commercial firm. In particular, pharmaceutical firms are active in biomedical research and the drug development area. Not only do such firms maintain their own laboratories, but many of them also sponsor research in the medical schools and universities under contractual agreements.

The development of new medicines is an activity that takes place in a web of organizational linkages. Individual citizens can influence these processes, but the influence is usually more effective when the organizations are confronted by people who have banded together in a group. Likewise, action is most effective when citizens are familiar with the ways that medical knowledge has evolved, the way medicines work, and the operating procedures of all the types of participating organizations.

2
The Early Plant Hunters

People have been hunting for and using plants for thousands and thousands of years. Indeed, there are early records of medicinal plants and the remedies made from them. An image on the wall of an early Egyptian tomb shows men presenting a variety of exotic plants to a pharaoh. A clay tablet from ancient Mesopotamia, known to be more than 4,000 years old, contains the oldest record of medical prescriptions. An Egyptian papyrus, written about 500 years later, provides recipes for medicinal compounds made from plants. Ancient Chinese scholars also contributed to the store of knowledge. A Chinese emperor in the third century B.C. discovered many new medicines—some of which are still in use.

The ancient Greeks acquired their medical information from these earlier civilizations and added new techniques and medicines of their own. The Romans accepted and further expanded this learning. Throughout the Greek and Roman times, the ancient tradition of collecting and identifying plants was continued. Medicinal plants were identified and listed in scrolls and, later, in books for the use of scholars and medical practitioners.

After the fall of Rome in A.D. 476, however, learning and experimentation were all but forgotten. The works of philosophers, poets, and scientists were in danger of destruction from neglect. Waves of invaders from the border lands between Europe and Asia flowed into western Europe. Governmental and other institutions collapsed or were abandoned. Precious writings were saved by two groups of people. In the West, many monks and nuns who served the Christian church spent their lives copying and preserving the manuscripts. In the Muslim empire—especially along the northern coast of Africa and in Spain—the ancient learning was transcribed and protected by Islamic, Jewish, and Christian scholars. During the Middle Ages (ca. 500 to ca. 1500), medical scholars from the Muslim-dominated areas greatly increased the store of medical knowledge—especially in the fields of chemistry and medicinal products.

After 711, when Islamic armies invaded and conquered Spain, learned Muslim Arabs, Jews, and Christians joined to forge a golden age in Spain. These scholars—aided by the religious tolerance prevalent at that time and place—were responsible for great advances in the arts and sciences. Indeed, during those times, Spanish scientists had the most advanced knowledge of medicine and medical botany. This golden age began to wane in the 1100s when the Muslims turned against the Jews. At that time, Jewish scholars and physicians began to leave Spain and migrate to other countries. Later, when Muslim dominance was threatened by armies from central Europe and local Spanish knights, further migrations of learned scientists took place. Southern Italy was an attractive refuge. The new migrants made the Italian peninsula a stronghold of medical education and practice. As early as the 11th century, the Italian city of Salerno had became the home of the first full-fledged medical school in Europe. According to legend, the school was founded by four masters—a Western Christian, an Eastern Christian, a Jew, and a Muslim.

During the High Renaissance in Italy in the early to mid-1500s, a period of great intellectual productivity, botanical interest in foreign plants was centered on ornamentals, plants cultivated for beauty. By the 1500s, northern Europe was prosperous, and people wanted showy gardens. New medicinal plants were still of interest, but most people believed that their apothecaries—who bought and sold herbs—knew everything about curing patients.

Rauwolf, Plant Hunter

Some scientists, however, continued to seek out and investigate new medicinal plants. One such scientist was a German botanist and physician, Leonhard Rauwolf. Because of his medical training, he was able to document his findings in a scientific and systematic manner. Rauwolf was born in Bavaria about 1535. He did his preliminary studies at the University of Wittenberg, a school not far from Berlin. In 1560, he began his advanced medical training at the University of Montpelier in southern France. Montpelier was then the finest medical school in Europe, and he received a splendid education.

Rauwolf was born during the Renaissance—a historical period that lasted from the 1300s until the end of the 1500s. During the Renaissance—a word that means rebirth—Europeans rediscovered the classical knowledge of the Greeks and Romans. Rauwolf was required to study the works of ancient authors such as Socrates, Plato, and Aristotle. The works of these and other Greek writers had long ago been translated into Latin and Arabic. The ancient Greek and Roman works generated great interest in many areas of human concern—including the sciences. Scientific writings and the works of the early physicians, such as Hippocrates, Dioscorides (a master herbalist), and Galen (a renowned anatomist and herbalist) were in demand.

The works of these physicians were studied by all medical students. In keeping with the ancient medical theories, standard treatments were almost exclusively herbal—meaning they were derived from plants. However, diet restrictions, purging of the bowels, and bleeding by either mechanical means or by leeches were a part of many treatment programs.

European students of medicine in Rauwolf's day were well versed in the Bible as well as knowledgeable about classical learning. During their Bible study, they noted the mention of each medicinal plant or herbal treatment. Because of this, a typical student had a special interest in medical practices that had originated in the Holy Lands of the eastern Mediterranean area. This area includes Greece, Turkey, and the biblical lands that are now called Iraq, Syria, Lebanon, Saudi Arabia, Jordan, and Israel. In Rauwolf's time, the biblical lands were all ruled by the Ottoman emperor of Turkey.

Rauwolf, like his fellow students, easily combined his deep interest in religion with his scientific studies. Most students believed that herbal medicines and their beneficial effects were all part of God's plan. During his studies, Rauwolf developed a strong desire to visit the Holy Lands. He wanted to explore those areas of the Ottoman Empire that would confirm the written descriptions of biblical plants and their surroundings. Rauwolf also looked forward to a pilgrimage that would deepen his religious faith.

Rauwolf's plans could not be fulfilled for several years. He knew that he must complete his medical studies before he could explore foreign lands. While applying himself to this task, he spent his free time investigating the botanical specimens found in the area of rural France near his medical school. Rauwolf's field trips netted a collection of 443 specimens, which he dried and mounted on white paper. Today, this collection can be seen at the museum of the University of Leyden (Leiden) in Holland.

In 1563, Rauwolf completed his medical education and looked forward to opening a medical practice in Augsburg, Germany. Two years later, he married Regina Jung, the daughter of a prominent Augsburg physician. In the next few years, Rauwolf twice moved his practice to other towns. In 1570, he and his family returned to Augsburg, and the city officials gave Rauwolf a yearly stipend to serve as a public health adviser. During these years, Rauwolf retained his interest in botany. He cultivated both rare plants and medicinal herbs with which to treat his patients.

For a long time, Rauwolf had desired to observe and collect plant specimens in their native surroundings. In 1572, when he was in his 30s, he decided to travel to the Holy Lands. To fulfill this ambition, however, he needed to find a source of financial support. Rauwolf's brother-in-law owned a trading company that did business in the Near East and was able to supply that support. He employed Rauwolf to act as physician to the company's representatives in that area. The brother-in-law hoped that Rauwolf could keep the employees in good health and perhaps discover plants that might prove valuable to the trading company. At that time, the idea of generating profit as a direct result of scientific study was an unusual concept. Historians believe that Rauwolf's arrangement might have been the first of its kind.

In the 1500s, France under King Francis I was the only European country to have a trade agreement with Suleiman, the Ottoman Turkish ruler. By the provisions of the treaty, France was allowed to extend its trading rights with the Ottoman Empire to any interested European citizen. The Germans who hired Rauwolf thus did business in the Mideast under the protection of the French.

On September 2, 1573, Rauwolf sailed from Marseille, France, for the city of Tripoli in present-day Lebanon. After more than three long weeks at sea, the travelers arrived near Tripoli.

The city of Tripoli, built on the slopes of Mount Lebanon, is some distance from the port. By the time Rauwolf and the others reached the city gates, the night curfew was in effect, and they were arrested. They were accused of trying to set the city afire with their lanterns. Fortunately, the French consul was passing the gate, and the German traders were released into his custody.

At first, Rauwolf and his companions found Tripoli to be a cramped and unattractive city. However, they soon found that the outside of the houses—with their windowless walls and small doorways—were very different from the inside. The walls often hid expansive gardens, beautiful patios with fountains, and attractive inner rooms.

The city was a busy transit point for goods sent from distant places such as India and China. Tripoli was also a major silk production center. Years before, large colonies of silkworms

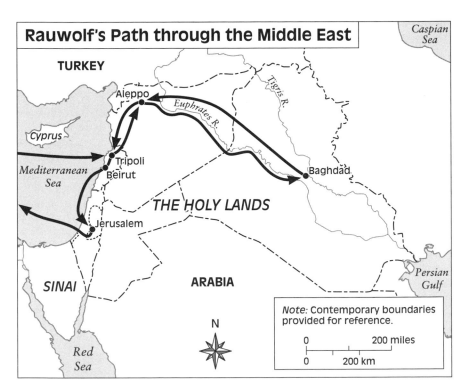

This map shows the routes taken by Rauwolf from Tripoli to Aleppo and on to Baghdad and back.

had been imported from China. Mulberry trees, also imported from China, were grown locally to feed the silkworms.

After about five weeks in Tripoli, Rauwolf was ready to move on. He had enjoyed seeing the various ornamental plants and learning about mulberry culture. Now, he wanted to begin his serious study of plant life and visit the Holy Lands. Company business dictated that the German traders' next stop would be the city of Aleppo. This ancient city, some miles west of the Euphrates River, is in northern Syria near the modern border with Turkey. Aleppo had long been a trading center with commerce in spices, cloth, precious stones, gold, and silver.

Rauwolf started his exploration of the area as quickly as possible, and two important plants were brought to his attention. He immediately began an investigation of Chinese sarsaparilla and Iranian rhubarb. He learned that the sarsaparilla plant helps cure venereal disease and that the roots of Iranian rhubarb are a remedy for many intestinal disorders and liver complaints. In addition to medicinal plants, Rauwolf studied other useful plants. He was the first European to describe the preparation of coffee and the Arabs' use of coffee on social occasions.

While in the area of Aleppo, Rauwolf collected many plants that were foreign to Europe. He remained there for nine months and then began the dangerous journey to Baghdad. Rauwolf and his companions traveled east from Aleppo to the headwaters of the Euphrates River. Next, they sailed down the Euphrates in a southeasterly direction toward the place nearest to Baghdad. That city lay about 100 land miles (160 km) east of this point on the western bank of the Tigris River.

Each evening on their voyage down the Euphrates, the crew pulled into shore and made camp. Even if he was tired, Rauwolf explored every campsite for new plants. However, good finds were scarce in the arid climate along the northern reaches of the Euphrates River. Some of his best finds were interesting species of gourds. When the gourds were dried and pulverized,

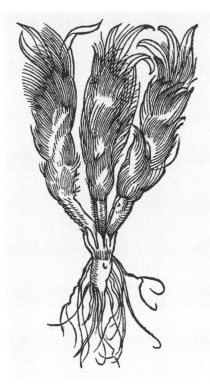

Plant names in the past were not always consistent. What the Europeans called nardus is probably the same plant mentioned in the Bible as spikenard. This plant was among those sought by Rauwolf in the Holy Lands.
(Courtesy of the Photographic Archive Services, National Library of Medicine)

the powder provided material for a strong laxative.

For the last leg of the journey to Baghdad, they left the relative ease of river travel. Much of the 100-mile (160-km) trip between the two rivers was through stark desert. Deserts are often difficult to travel through, but Rauwolf's main worry was a possible encounter with Bedouin tribespeople who were unhappy with the rule of the Turkish sultan.

The group eventually arrived safely at their destination on the Tigris River. They found the area around Baghdad to be quite fertile because it received irrigation from the river. In this well-cultivated area, Rauwolf found few plants that were unknown to the Europeans. After a short stay, the party prepared to return to Aleppo by a land route. Rauwolf and his companions joined a caravan and traveled by horseback in a northerly direction for hundreds of miles up the east bank of the Tigris River. They then proceeded westward until they reached Aleppo.

The travelers received bad news when they reached Aleppo. Rauwolf's brother-in-law's trading company was bankrupt and the company's representatives in Tripoli were being held in prison. Although the rest of his party continued on, Rauwolf decided to remain for a time in Aleppo. To support himself, he became the family physician to the many resident European traders.

Rauwolf's final adventure in the Ottoman Empire was a trip to Jerusalem, the heart of the Holy Lands. At that time, wars and political unrest had left the city in poor condition. Rauwolf was disappointed with this situation and remained in Jerusalem for a very short time. While there, he continued his collecting and found a few unusual plants in the area.

It was now time to return to Augsburg. Rauwolf experienced several further adventures during his journey home. On his sea voyage, he successfully avoided pirates and bad weather. During high winter, Rauwolf safely crossed the dangerous Brenner Pass in the Swiss Alps. He arrived in Augsburg on February 12, 1576, two years and six months after his departure from Marseille.

All in all, Rauwolf's ventures were successful. He benefited from the fame brought by the publication of his memoirs. His collection of 364 preserved plant species from the Middle East was a major contribution to the botanical studies of the time. Consequently, Rauwolf gained a high reputation within the community of botanical scholars. Indeed by the time he died in 1596, the story of his life had reached legendary status.

Rauwolf's story did not end with his death. More than 100 years later, in the early 1700s, Europeans were thoroughly exploring the Americas. Plant hunters in the Caribbean area discovered many slightly different varieties of known types of plants. However, some of the specimens appeared to belong to a previously unknown group. The German who found the new type decided to name it in honor of Rauwolf. The newly discovered type of plants became the genus *Rauwolfia*.

Over the next 150 years, the story of *Rauwolfia* became increasingly complicated. Botanists uncovered many new plants within the new genus named after Rauwolf. Members of this genus—a related group of plants—grow wild in all tropical or semitropical zones. In fact, members of the genus were seen to prosper under a wide variety of soil and moisture conditions.

Reserpine

In India, one species of *Rauwolfia* had been used for centuries to treat snakebite. This use probably originated because the root of the plant resembles a snake. Native healers often linked the treatment of a disease to a medicinal plant that somehow resembled the cause of the illness. In this case, the snakebite patient was given the ground or powdered snake-shaped root of the rauwolfia plant.

Another traditional Indian use of powdered rauwolfia root was to ease mental disorders. Probably this use was discovered accidentally when a person with mental problems was given a dose of the root for a snakebite. The attending healer might have noted its effectiveness in calming the patient. European physicians in the 1700s, however, were unimpressed with any substance that they regarded as a folk remedy. They did not try this treatment to calm mentally ill patients.

Rauwolfia, *or Indian snakeroot, has been used in folk medicine as a treatment for snakebite, but it is far more important as a source of reserpine, an effective, natural tranquilizer.* (Courtesy of the New York Botanical Garden)

Although rauwolfia was long recognized in the official Indian list of drugs, it received no Western-style scientific investigation until the 1930s. Then, Indian physicians and biochemists, trained in European methods, began to take an interest in the plant. The results of their controlled studies showed convincingly that the rauwolfia powder was an effective tranquilizer. Their findings gave European scientists new incentives for further investigations. In 1952, a German chemist isolated the active ingredient, an alkaloid he called reserpine. With the pure drug to study, it soon became evident that small doses could effect a profound change in the behavior of agitated psychiatric patients. An hour or so after treatment, the patients became calm and untroubled. This condition allowed patients to respond to other forms of psychotherapy, including psychoanalysis. Equally important, it was found that negative side effects were few if the drug was administered properly. Reserpine was seen to be a natural tranquilizer.

The main source of the drug is *Rauwolfia serpentina*, a short, shrublike plant that belongs to the same family as the periwinkle—also known for its medicinal properties. This member of the genus *Rauwolfia* has become far more important than any of the nearly 400 plants that Rauwolf found on his trip to the lands of the Bible.

Its importance in the treatment of mental illness can only be understood when compared to treatment that it replaced. It is particularly useful in the treatment of agitated depression where treatments once included electroshock therapy and convulsive therapy induced by the administration of large doses of insulin. Now, almost 50 years after the adoption of reserpine in conventional medical practices, there are many alternative tranquilizers—some more effective than reserpine. Today, mentally disturbed people often receive reserpine in combination with other medicines. This treatment seeks to promote the total well-being of the patient.

3
The Framework of Folk Medicine

In industrial societies, most people visit a trained caregiver when they need medical treatment. Usually, the caregiver has been qualified for that position under strict regulations. These health-care providers have completed a lengthy, prescribed program of education and training in their chosen fields. They have been trained as physical therapists, nurse practitioners, cancer specialists, family physicians, or in any one of a long list of specialties. At the completion of their programs, they are tested on their knowledge and understanding of the principles of health care. After passing rigorous tests, each care provider receives a license to enter into professional practice.

The provider may establish a solo practice and offer health-care services as an independent professional. Increasingly, however, qualified people accept positions in a setting where care is provided by a team of professionals who represent a wide range of specialties.

Not all people seek medical help from a professional caregiver. Indeed, people may decide to practice self-care for a variety of health considerations. One example is the person who decides to stop smoking or chewing tobacco. Other modes of self-care typically involve dieting or following a program of physical exercises. However, the most common self-care practice is the use of nonprescription medicines such as aspirin, antacid remedies, and lotions for treating muscle aches or skin conditions. Many herbal remedies, sold as dietary supplements rather than medicines, are also self-prescribed to restore or improve health.

Folk medicine offers several alternatives to those who do not choose to seek a licensed caregiver. Some people may decide to prepare their own medicines from herbs. Recipes for the preparation of such medicines can be found in books available at public libraries and bookstores. Medicinal plants grow wild in woods or fields, and they can be planted in home gardens. However, descriptions of the wild plants are often somewhat vague. This leads to the unfortunate prospect that the untrained person will pick the wrong plant. Mushrooms are especially difficult to identify from descriptions in books. Usually, the recipes caution an inexperienced person to avoid the use of certain potentially dangerous plant materials. A cautious person may not want to attempt making certain medicines and may seek a folk healer with an established reputation.

Today, those who practice folk medicine use many natural plant products to treat their patients. Medicinal plants are part of a health-care tradition that has been passed from generation to generation. Because of this, the various powders, liquids, and ointments made from these plants are frequently called traditional medicines.

Traditional medicine began with the first human communities. Over time, humans learned about the food and medical value of plants by using a trial-and-error method. Wrapping a bleeding wound with large leaves might have been the first therapeutic use of plant material. When this primitive bandage proved to be successful, it became a standard method to treat wounds. An observant clan member might have noted that certain plant leaves speeded healing. Eventually, that plant might have been given a distinctive name and designated to be used as a dressing for injuries. The discovery of a beneficial plant is a positive outcome of a trial-and-error experience.

However, the use of the wrong plant might be fatal. When such an error resulted in a death, clan members would attempt to identify the cause. Eventually, perhaps after a series of similar deaths, the poisonous plant would be identified and the knowledge of its effects would be passed on to others.

Humans often assigned special powers to deadly plants. They reasoned that if the full power of the plant could sicken and kill a human, perhaps a small amount of the plant's power could destroy an illness. Further trial and error sometimes led to a successful use of such potent materials. Today, those scientists who search for medicinal plants often use a similar strategy. They also believe that a plant with a strong biological effect—even a poison—might have medicinal properties.

In their search for foods and remedies, humans found the consumption of some plants to be disagreeable but not deadly. Others were found to cause mild stomach upset or vomiting, while still others caused severe cramps and violent intestinal problems. People learned to avoid these unpleasant plants or used them to purge—or rid—the body of more deadly materials.

In addition to plants that acted as purges, people in preindustrial societies found that certain plant materials relieved pain, provided unusual energy, or caused visions of strange colors and objects. These people reasoned that if plants could bring on such beneficial or extraordinary effects, the plants might be gifts from the gods. The use of such plants in religious ceremonies developed. They continue today among some groups. Participants in these religious ceremonies—such as those followed by some clans in the Amazon regions—ingest plant material to induce visions. The worshipers believe that such revelations expand their religious experiences.

Traditional healers have long been guided by a set of ideas as they select their medicinal plants. Some of these ideas include the principle of "signatures." Healers believe that if

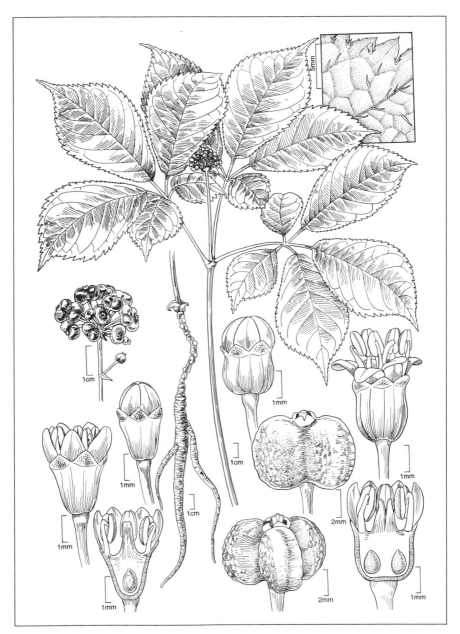

Extracts of the ginseng root have been used for centuries as a general tonic, first in China and now all over the world. (Courtesy of Alice Tangerini and the Smithsonian Institution)

some part of a plant resembles an organ of the human body, the medicinal value of that plant will be directed toward that specific organ. In other words, if the flower of a plant resembles a heart, medicine made from the plant is thought to bring relief for heart disease.

This theory is common throughout the world. For many centuries, the Chinese have regarded the root of the ginseng plant as an important medicine. This stems from the idea that the root resembles a human body in miniature. Consequently, powdered ginseng root is thought to increase the health and vigor of the entire body. Today, the use of powdered ginseng has become popular in Western cultures.

Another kind of signature plant is thought to resemble the cause of an illness and, therefore, is used to cure that illness. One example of this is the use of a species of the *Rauwolfia* plant, whose root looks like a snake, to cure snakebite.

Some folk healers believe that the area in which a disease is prevalent supports the plant that cures the disease; this is known as colocation. Consequently, people were not surprised when the cinchona tree was found in tropical regions where malaria is common. The bark of this tree produces the medicine quinine, which relieves the fevers of malaria, a tropical disease transmitted by the *Anopheles* mosquito.

In this case, the idea about location seemed to be verified. However, the effectiveness of a medicine has nothing to do with its appearance or the place where it grows. Indeed, for many years, the cinchona tree would not thrive in India, the region where malaria is most prevalent.

Although signatures and the idea of colocation proved to be invalid, the trial-and-error method uncovered many natural medicines. Over the centuries, positive results occurred because healers were willing to test almost every plant, note the successes and failures, and pass on their findings to others. This persistence—and some good luck—has given folk medicine practitioners many treatments that are still in use.

Today, scientists often consult with tribal shamans when seeking new medicinal plants in regions such as tropical rain forests. They also study the lifestyles of preindustrial people to gain information about local plants. The discovery of curare in the rain forests of South America is a classic example of such a study. In this area, native people hunted with blowguns and curare-covered darts. Curare, a poisonous drug made from a vine, paralyzes its prey. Explorers saw the effects of curare as a possible treatment for severe agitation—such as an epileptic seizure. Although that usage was found to be impractical, curare later proved to be a valuable muscle relaxant when employed in anesthesia. In general, if a plant exhibits any intense biological effects, scientists attempt to isolate and study the active ingredients as a possible treatment for disease.

In the practice of folk medicine, ideas such as plant signatures are shared across cultural boundaries and over time and space. However, the great diversity found in traditional medicine is caused by differences in local diseases, native plants, and cultural practices.

The Influences of Native Americans

The idea of rigorous tests for health-care procedures was not introduced until the early 1900s. In the 1500s, during the first exchanges in North America between native peoples and Europeans, medications and treatments used on both sides of the Atlantic lacked any type of control. European practitioners often used in their medicines what many would consider truly unpleasant ingredients—such as dried excrement and pulverized sexual organs of animals. Similar materials were employed by the native peoples of North and South America.

The story of an early cultural encounter illustrates the nature of the exchange between two prescientific cultures. In late 1535, the French explorer Jacques Cartier began his expedition up the St. Lawrence River of what is now Canada. Because of various delays, he did not reach the vicinity of present-day Montreal until winter had arrived. After a few weeks, his ships were immobilized by ice. The crew was soon low on rations and began to show the symptoms of scurvy, a life-threatening vitamin deficiency. At that time, no one understood the cause and treatment of this disease. One hundred men—out of the crew of 110—were unfit for duty by February 1536.

The diary of one of Cartier's crew members relates that a local Iroquois leader became very ill from scurvy. The Frenchmen were surprised when the man appeared to be fully cured a few days later. Cartier observed that the Iroquois women brewed a mixture of juniper needles and bark and gave the tea to those who were ill. The dregs of the brew were used to bathe the legs of the afflicted men. When the Frenchmen were offered this treatment, they disliked the strong smell of the tea and at first refused to try it. Finally, some consented to drink the concoction and were soon relieved of their symptoms. Although the sailors did not understand the reason, the scurvy was cured by the vitamin C found in the needles of the juniper tree. The Europeans had unknowingly obtained the needed vitamin by drinking the brew. Bathing the legs did nothing for the sufferers—except make them smell like a pine tree.

This story is often told as one example of an effective folk medicine. Although the Iroquois did use the juniper mash in a medically effective manner, this remedy appears to be another outcome of the trial-and-error method rather than a treatment derived from a true understanding of the illness.

Both the Iroquois and the French thought scurvy was a disease transmitted by physical contact. The French medical procedure was simply to avoid being near anyone who showed the symptoms. The Iroquois hoped to relieve the ill effects of the contagious disease by serving the juniper tea. Neither the

French nor the Iroquois had a true idea of the cause of the disease or the reason why the treatment worked.

Native American medical practices, such as the medicinal use of juniper needles, varied from tribe to tribe and region to region. Many of these practices were closely allied to religious convictions that included a belief in supernatural powers. Indeed, the native priest, or shaman, often recited incantations or prayers over the body of the patient. This alliance between medicine, superstition, and religion was similar to European concepts in the 16th through the 19th centuries.

During the early 1700s, some English colonists adopted the use of local medicinal plants when they were unable to obtain their usual medicines. For example, they followed the Indians' lead and used tobacco as a cure for various ailments. Ironically, the conditions treated included lung congestion. In contrast, other settlers did not trust the Native American remedies and made their own preparations from local medicinal plants. The Puritan settlers in New England went even further. They refused to use any local remedies and imported all their curative ingredients from London.

While some spread of knowledge and practice did occur, neither Europeans nor Native

Native Americans used tobacco primarily in ceremonies. Europeans adopted tobacco as a health aid and later as a recreational drug. (Courtesy of the Photographic Archive Services, National Library of Medicine)

Native Americans used the roots of the wild mayapple to combat intestinal worms. Researchers are testing the active ingredients for possible use against cancer. (Courtesy of Monica S. and Timothy B. Guenther)

Americans shared all of their health-care information. The prejudices of the settlers and the reluctance of Native Americans to reveal the details of their tribal practices prevented much cultural exchange.

The Native American contribution to modern medicine is difficult to evaluate. However, it is helpful to note the actual number of Indian remedies accepted by physicians in the United States. In the 1800s, United States Pharmacopoeia, an official list of drugs made from medicinal plants, included 200 Native American remedies. When the new laws on safety and effectiveness were put into practice in the 1920s, many traditional remedies—including many of Indian origin—were removed from the list. Today, only 13 North American Indian remedies remain in official use. Even garlic—a time-honored medicine—was dropped in 1936. Interestingly, processed garlic is now a popular food supplement that some believe has health-giving properties.

Of the Indian remedies accepted in the 1800s, a few powerful laxatives, such as extracts of the mayapple, and some rubs and ointments are still in use. Perhaps the most valuable are wintergreen and witch hazel, important external medicines for soothing aching muscles. Other native materials still in use have undergone radical changes in function. Cornstarch, once used as a remedy for poisoning, is now a component in bath powders. Wild cherry extract, a flavoring agent to hide the unpleasant taste of strong medicine, was previously a popular cough remedy.

Plant remedies from South America have also been used by traditional folk healers on both American continents. Products from some of these plants—kola nut extract, cayenne pepper, and ground arrowroot—are now used as flavorings in food or drink. Powdered papain, once an important drug, is now used as a meat tenderizer. Today, cochineal, made by drying and grinding certain insects, is a red coloring agent. However, four significant South American drugs continue to be used as internal medicines. These are quinine, cocaine, curare, and ipecac.

These four medicinal substances made from South American plants have been important to modern health care. Quinine, the first effective drug employed in the treatment of malaria, has saved millions of lives in many regions of the world. (Although it has now been replaced by other, more powerful malaria drugs, for years quinine was the only treatment.) In some places, cocaine is utilized in eye examinations to dilate the pupil of the eye. Curare is an ingredient in anesthetics. The powdered root of the ipecac plant is used in a syrup to induce vomiting. The syrup can be safely administered to children who have swallowed poison.

While a few medicinal plants from North and South America are still used to cure or alleviate major health problems, many

The ipecac plant's roots produce a juice that causes severe vomiting. Combined with sugar water, the juice makes syrup that can be given to children to induce vomiting. This is useful when a child has accidentally swallowed a toxic substance. (Courtesy of the New York Botanical Garden)

of the natural remedies used in the past have been found to have little real merit. Nevertheless, during the 20th century, members of the scientific community as well as practitioners of folk medicine continue to search for medicinal plants that will help the sick.

Modern Folk Practitioners

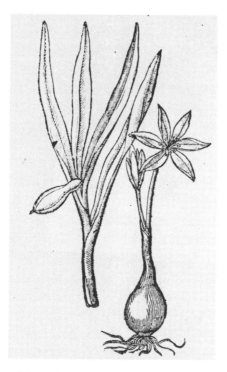

Although the meadow saffron plant is poisonous to humans and animals, the juice from its seeds and roots has been used as a treatment for gout, a disorder of the urinary system. (Courtesy of the Photographic Archive Services, National Library of Medicine)

In recent years, scientists have sought out and interviewed folk practitioners in the United States and shamans in remote places such as the Amazon jungle as part of their search for new medicinal plants. The scientists hope to acquire information about unknown medicinal plants and health-care practices before this knowledge is lost in the press of modern life.

Integration of Old and New Practices

In Western Europe, traditional medicine is more integrated into mainstream health care than it is in the United States. In France and the United Kingdom, the use of herbal remedies is an established practice. In these countries,

Portions of the coneflower known as echinacea are used to strengthen the body's defenses against infections. The plant is related to the black-eyed Susan. (Courtesy of James Manhart, Texas A&M University)

the effectiveness of such materials is not tested by the government. Physicians prescribe and pharmacists dispense traditional remedies that have been in use for many years. There is still a strong traditional element in these practices.

Before herbal compounds can be dispensed as medicines in Germany, they are tested for safety and effectiveness. However, many of these products cannot be sold as medicines in the United States. A prime example is the genus *Echinacea*. The juice of this plant is said to contain chemicals that may activate the body's own defenses against many different infections. Echinacea is sold as a dietary supplement—not a medicine—in the United States.

Other products popular in Germany include ginkgo extract, chamomile tincture, and the powdered leaves of the feverfew plant. Many similar materials have been approved for health care by a German government commission.

In Germany, the commercial value of such health-care products has become increasingly important. Indeed, the cultivation of the herbs, the extraction of the active ingredients, the packaging of the products, and the marketing of the remedies are directed by industrial firms that specialize in this technology.

These products are designated as dietary supplements in the United States. Commercial trade in dietary supplements is now the principal source of herbal medicines. The U.S. Food and Drug Administration (FDA) oversees some aspects of this commercial activity, such as product labeling. The FDA regulates dietary supplements by requiring accurate labeling and restricting unproved health claims.

An agency of the United Nations, the Food and Agricultural Organization (FAO) is active in international negotiations that are concerned with dietary supplements. The organization works toward international rules and regulations for these products that are in agreement with the rules and regulations of each member country. In addition, the FAO promotes identical labeling practices on all products sold as dietary supplements in international trade.

In 2004, the World Health Organization adopted a similar program for alternative or traditional medical treatments. The goal is to standardize the regulation of nonconventional practices in all countries.

4
How Medicines Work

Medicines are chemical compounds. Many people are disturbed when they hear the word *chemical* because they think of poisons and pollutants. However not only are all medicines chemicals, all foods, natural as well as synthetic, are made of chemicals. In fact, all human bodies are made entirely of chemicals. Without chemicals there would be no medicines, no food—and indeed, no life.

The basic unit of chemistry is the atom, a tiny particle of matter that cannot be further broken down and still remain that element. At present, chemists have identified 90 naturally occurring elements and 21 synthetically formed types. The 90 atoms are the elements that make up everything naturally occurring on Earth. Each of the elements has been assigned a special name and an abbreviation of that name.

Two or more atoms joined together form a molecule. Molecules may be composed of atoms of one single element or atoms of two or more different elements. For example, oxygen (O) is an element. The air humans breathe is composed of the molecular form of oxygen, which is two atoms of oxygen joined together (O_2). Water molecules are made of two atoms of the element hydrogen (H_2) and one atom of the element oxygen (O). The chemical composition (formula) of water is written as H_2O. The small number, or subscript, refers to the number of atoms of each element in the molecule.

Except for water and a few other materials used in very small amounts, all molecules made and used by living organisms contain the element carbon (C). Carbon, like oxygen, can bond with itself (C_2). When it does so, it forms a crystal-like structure that does not support life. Both diamonds and graphite, the material used as pencil lead, are carbon in crystal form. Life-giving, carbon-based molecules always include other elements such as hydrogen and oxygen. Most medicines contain carbon-based molecules. These carbon-based molecules often include other elements such as nitrogen (N), sulfur (S), Iron (Fe), and magnesium (Mg).

The Cell

The tissues and organs of plants and animals are composed of thousands of tiny cells. The cell is the basic unit of biology. Each cell has a wall or membrane that keeps it intact and separate from other cells. The cell is the place where diseases strike. For example, infectious diseases may occur when microbes such as bacteria or viruses invade the cell. The action of the microbes can kill the cells, and the death of the cells may result in the symptoms of the disease.

In some diseases such as diabetes, the cells of particular organs fail to function properly. Specifically, in diabetes, cells in the organ called the pancreas fail to produce an enzyme called insulin that keeps the proper level of sugar in the blood. Some diabetic patients must add insulin to their bloodstream by injection.

When body cells reproduce so rapidly that their growth prevents other cells from functioning, the condition is known as cancer. The onset of cancer means that something has gone wrong with the chemical processes within the cancerous cell.

Living cells are remarkably active chemical factories. In the space of a few minutes, a living cell can disassemble and reassemble thousands of molecules. The chemical action of a cell causes the atoms within the cell to group together to form new parts for that cell or for other cells. The cessation or disruption of this work is a basic cause of disease.

The construction of sugar molecules is the main activity of plant cells. Sugar molecules are made from carbon dioxide, which is composed of one carbon atom and two oxygen atoms, (CO_2) and water (H_2O). Plant cells use the Sun's energy to break apart the molecules of carbon dioxide and water in order to build sugar molecules. The plant captures some of the Sun's energy and stores it in each molecule of sugar.

After the sugar molecules are manufactured, some are joined together in chains to form starch. In turn, some of the starch chains link together to form cellulose. The energy in the sugar molecules is available to the plant for immediate use. However, the energy in the starch chains is stored for future use. For example, the starch stored in a seed will supply the energy for its underground growth. The longer cellulose chains are employed as the raw material for the assembly and repair of cell walls.

Plant cells manufacture other materials in addition to sugar, starch, and cellulose. The simplest compounds are vegetable oils. Some oils are long, straight chains of carbon and hydrogen atoms. In other vegetable oils, these straight chains have added side chains of various lengths.

Some substances are formed of carbon atoms joined in a circle or ring. The simplest of these ring-shaped molecules is called benzene. In 1825, Michael Faraday, a British scientist, isolated this compound when he was distilling a residue of whale oil. The benzene did not react with other chemicals in the expected manner. Faraday was curious about the unusual material and studied it further. However, he was unable to determine the exact structure of the molecules.

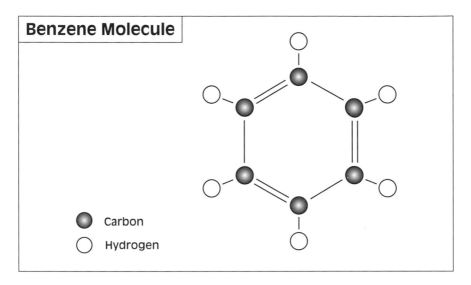

Benzene Molecule

- ● Carbon
- ○ Hydrogen

The benzene molecule is formed by six carbon atoms. One hydrogen atom is attached to each carbon atom. The benzene molecule is a building block for many important medicines.

In 1865, the German chemist Friedrich Kekule attempted to identify the true structure of benzene. While deliberating on this problem, he supposedly had a prophetic dream. It is said that he dreamed of six snakes, each biting the tail of the one ahead and forming a perfect circle. Whether this story is true or not, Kekule later proved that benzene is a flat ring of six carbon atoms. Today, scientists know that benzene rings are key components of many important plant medicines.

Although carbon, oxygen, and hydrogen are essential to all living things, other elements are also important to life. Some of the most interesting molecules are composed of nitrogen attached to carbon rings or other carbon structures. These molecules are called proteins. Plant cells build protein to serve many purposes, such as binding together the cellulose chains to form the cell walls.

A special class of proteins is called enzymes. In addition to nitrogen, enzymes may contain sulfur, magnesium, copper, or iron. Enzymes are catalysts, substances that activate or regulate chemical reactions but are, themselves, unchanged by the reactions.

Chlorophyll, the green plant enzyme, contains magnesium and utilizes the Sun's rays to produce sugar. All plant leaves are filled with chlorophyll, and most have acquired the green color of the enzyme. The amazing manner in which the magnesium in leaves helps to capture the Sun's energy remains somewhat mysterious.

The element iron is in the enzyme hemoglobin, a component of red blood cells. Iron is a vital ingredient because it absorbs oxygen from the air we breathe. The hemoglobin then carries the life-sustaining oxygen to all parts of the body.

Enzymes activate many important processes in cells—such as the complicated production of proteins. To do this vital work, enzymes must link several specific molecules. Without the enzyme, the molecules would float past one another in the liquid inside the cell. To initiate protein production, the enzyme fits into one of the specific molecules like a key into a lock. The protruding end of the "key" acts as a hook to catch a different specific molecule; after this linkage, the reaction between the two molecules can take place.

Enzymes and Medicines

Diseases can be caused by a shortage of a particular enzyme. In some cases, a medicine can substitute for the missing enzyme and help cure the disease. For example, in the disease called epilepsy, there is a shortage of enzyme that control the connections between nerve cells in the brain and nerve cells that control the muscles. For many years, scientists have searched for the correct mixture of enzymes that will prevent the symptoms of epilepsy without reducing the normal activity of the brain. Their goal is to find a replacement for the missing enzymes.

Some diseases are caused by bacterial infection. These infectious bacteria produce foreign enzymes after invading the body. Medicines can link with the foreign molecules, interfere with the function of the invading microbes, and limit the effects of the disease.

The Chemical Source of Plant Medicines

Some plant cells produce strange enzymelike molecules that do not contribute to the productive work of plant cells. Since scientists tend to believe that everything in nature has a purpose, they are curious to discover the use of these unusual enzymes. They now believe that the strange molecules might be part of a plant's defense system. Some of the molecules have a bitter taste and others are poisonous. Perhaps these mysterious chemicals help the plant ward off its enemies. Scientists hope that some of these bitter or poisonous enzymes can be used as medicines.

Today, medical researchers are able to adjust the dosage of a medicine containing poisonous enzymes so that only selected cells are killed. Scientists can also redesign the molecules of these enzymes to kill cancer cells but allow healthy cells to survive.

Specific Case Studies

THE VINCA DRUGS

The discovery of the curative powers of the rosy periwinkle was the outcome of a series of remarkably lucky accidents. The sequence began through the actions of a Canadian physician, Clark Noble, who specialized in treating diabetes. His interest in diabetes had risen during his doctoral training, 30 years previously, when he had worked on pioneering efforts to extract the insulin that could control diabetes symptoms from the internal organs of fish such as cod. While technically successful, these efforts were ignored or derided by the medical authorities and were finally dropped for lack of support. Such an outcome led Noble to shift his professional interests from research to clinical practice.

In the early 1950s, one of his diabetic patients was visiting Jamaica and encountered a locally popular home remedy based on a tea made from the dried, ground leaves of the periwinkle, a perennial shrub sometimes called myrtle. The patient sent a packet of the dried leaves to Noble's medical office in Toronto. Noble was willing to go along with the patient's ideas but was long past the capability of performing the proper laboratory tests needed to establish the value of the tealike concoction. However, he was still interested in supporting new—or even radical—ways to treat diabetes. Consequently, he sent the packet to his brother, Robert L. Noble, who was doing biochemical research at the University of Western Ontario.

When tested by Robert, the extract showed no effect on the level of glucose in the blood and was deemed useless for the treatment of diabetes. However, the chemical analyses also revealed that the infusion contained a host of biologically active substances. With the help of a research colleague from the University of British Columbia, Charles T. Beer, Robert isolated a crucial alkaloid in the mix and named it vincristine.

Vincristine tested well against cancer cells in the laboratory and by 1959, clinical trials revealed that it was very effective against childhood leukemia. In a short time the recovery rate from this disease went from a meager 20 percent to an encouraging 80 percent of cases. Other developments followed.

Vinblastine was soon isolated and proved effective against breast cancer and other disorders.

THE TAXOL DRUGS

As health-care providers and biomedical researchers became aware of the success of these two plant-derived products, interest in large-scale botanical surveys began to increase. The intermittent survey and specimen collection work that had been underway at the U.S. Department of Agriculture (USDA) for many decades was about to be expanded and given a change of focus. By the early 1960s, officials of the National Cancer Institute (NCI) and the USDA had agreed about a project whereby botanists and coworkers from the USDA would conduct plant surveys and collect large numbers of specimens while employees of the NCI would conduct tests of medical effectiveness. In addition, the directors of the NCI established connections with leaders in biomedical research at various colleges and universities and, in turn, with various pharmaceutical firms. The idea was to create a pipeline for medicinal products from the forests and prairies to the local drugstore.

One of the plant materials collected by the field workers was bark from the Pacific yew, an evergreen that grows as a large shrub in the pine forests in Oregon and Washington. In the summer of 1962, Arthur Barclay, a USDA field botanist, sent a package of the dried bark to Monroe Wall at the Research Triangle Institute in North Carolina. Wall, a biochemist specializing in the analysis of natural products, was supervising the research done under contract for the NCI. For several years prior to moving to the Research Triangle Institute, Wall had worked with some limited success on the composition of possible anticancer materials from a tree native to China and Tibet and known to European botanists as *Camptotheca acuminata*. Wall was eager to try his techniques on the new challenge. He and a colleague, M. C. Wani, spent many months of laborious fractionation work to isolate the key ingredient and spent still more time in determining the molecular structure of the active ingredient once it was purified. Using the most advanced analytical tools, such as magnetic resonance imaging, they were finally able to determine the molecule's basic structure by May 1971. The reason for the delay was the molecule's complexity. The main body of the molecule is made of three tightly adjacent carbon rings. This central feature has two armlike attachments of one carbon ring each—linked to the main body by chains made of two oxygen atoms in succession. The chemists named this odd molecule, taxol, signifying that it was an alcohol-type extract from the plant with the Latin name, *Taxus brevifolia*.

Preliminary tests indicated that the compound did kill cancer cells in a laboratory setting. However, a serious problem was looming. Thirty pounds of bark were needed to produce a mere pinch of taxol. If the material turned out to be effective against cancer in a clinical setting with human patients, the supply of yew bark might soon be exhausted. To complicate matters, the Pacific yew grows very slowly—reaching full maturity only after 200 years.

Environmental activists were generally aware of the bark-collecting work that had been undertaken by the big lumber and paper-making companies, who harvested the evergreen forests of the Northwest. By the mid-1970s, these activists were beginning to organize a movement to protect the Pacific yew from extinction. The officials of the National Cancer Institute recognized the prospective conflict. They were also concerned about cost. Collection of bark and the extraction of taxol were already costing millions of dollars, and the substance still had not even been approved for clinical trials. These problems led the officials at NCI to slow down the process of evaluation. In effect, taxol was put on the back burner for several months.

Further progress came from a new corner of the biosciences. Susan Horowitz, at Yeshiva University in New York, was a specialist in the microchemistry of the inside workings of bodily cells. She had some novel ideas about how anticancer compounds worked. She called upon her science colleagues at the NCI to provide her with a sample of taxol so that she could test her ideas in the laboratory. By 1981, she was able to show that taxol worked by overexciting the processes of chromosome organization in a cell that was about to divide. Fine strands of material are needed by the cell to make the division effective. Taxol caused a cell to overproduce these strands, thereby clogging the cell reproductive activity. Since cancer cells are engaged in rapid reproduction, taxol selectively attacked such cells.

This discovery energized the biomedical research community, and interest in taxol as an anticancer drug surged. Much more extensive animal tests were now in order, and clinical trials using human subjects were on the horizon. Indeed, these crucial tests were done, and the results were published in 1987. Taxol proved to be remarkably effective against ovarian cancer, and the compound was approved for prescription use by the U.S. Food and Drug Administration (FDA) in 1988.

The news aroused the environmentalists of Oregon and Washington. The movement that had begun in the 1970s and had lain fallow for several years was reenergized. The cost problem for the administrators at the NCI was also increasingly severe. Taxol production was costing the government about $250,000 a pound.

In this context, many enterprising scientists were thinking about the possibility of developing a synthetic version of taxol. However, building such a molecule from scratch in a process of total synthesis appeared unlikely. If pieces of the molecule could be found from natural sources, it might be possible to put the pieces together. Such a process is called a semisynthesis.

Fortunately, some French scientists had discovered an alternative source for the core unit in the taxol molecule. That part of the molecule was readily available in economical quantities from the English yew, cousin to the Pacific yew but far more commonplace. In fact, it is a widely used ornamental shrub and was coincidently growing in the hedge just outside the laboratory that housed the French research team. The needles from this common evergreen contain large amounts of the basic raw material.

The French researchers were making progress but struggling to achieve the proper linkages for the odd attachments on the basic molecule. Their procedure for doing so required about 60 steps of chemical manipulation so that production was very slow. Similarly, the final yield was very low, making each batch quite costly.

In spite of these remaining problems, it was time to activate the pharmaceutical production industry. A competition for a cooperative contract arrangement was initiated by the officials of the NCI. In 1989, a contract was awarded to the Bristol-Myers Squibb Corporation. They were prepared to try to improve on the French process and simultaneously undertake the animal tests and clinical trials that could lead to approval by the FDA.

A new player had already entered the scene in 1985. At that time, Robert Holton had just accepted an appointment as a professor of biochemistry at Florida State University in Tallahassee. He had been fascinated by taxol for some years and had done some preliminary studies to familiarize himself with the molecule's peculiarities. He was encouraged to apply to the NCI for a research grant specifically targeting the synthesis or partial synthesis of the taxol molecule.

Since the French discoveries were patented in the United States and were therefore open to study, Holton could build on what was already known. He just had to find a way to add the molecular pieces together more efficiently. He did so by using a metallic catalyst that cut the number of steps from 60 down to four, vastly improving the yield. The key was the use of a specially designed metal catalyst in a broth of molecular fragments. This procedure was promptly patented. So by 1989, Bristol-Myers Squibb executives were eager to enter into a profit-sharing agreement with the Florida State University and Robert Holton.

In 1992, the FDA approved the drug for the treatment of cancer. And in 1993, sufficient quantities were available for its release into the hands of cancer-care providers. The new drug was a major success and Bristol-Myers Squibb was able to charge almost $6,000 for a single dose. While this price raised serious questions on the part of health-care administrators and politicians, the company was able to justify its price based on the costs of the advanced test and development work that they had done.

Meanwhile, Holton continued to tinker productively with the basic molecule and brought several hundred new variations in the product under patent. He also patented several of the chemical procedures needed to modify such a complicated molecule.

THE WORMWOOD DRUGS

Trying a wide range of source materials or focusing on those that are known to have poisonous properties are two well-practiced strategies for finding new medicines. Another strategy is to use folk healers' practices as clues. In the case of the rosy periwinkle, the folk practices were not affirmed by further study. However, there have been several instances where the folk practices were verified *and* the drug developers were also led to discover even better outcomes.

The source material in this case is a special variety of wormwood. As the name suggests, extracts of wormwood foliage have been used through the ages to counter the effects of intestinal worms. In Europe, wormwood essence from a slightly different plant was mixed with other herbal materials in alcohol as a carrier. The idea was to clear the system of worms. The product is known as absinthe—now a prohibited drink because of its toxicity.

Archeological finds suggest that some form of wormwood tea was used in ancient Chinese medicine as a treatment for malaria. That application was borrowed from the bamboo scrolls recovered in the 1970s, and wormwood has become a valued supplement to other antimalarials—particularly in the face of declining effectiveness of the derivatives of quinine. This success in modern medicine led biomedical research workers at the University of Washington to study the details of the wormwood extract. The active ingredient was isolated and named Artemisinin. The scientists found that Artemisinin has a particular affinity for iron. The malaria parasite has an abundance of iron in its cellular plasma. The drug acts with the iron content in a way that breaks down the cell membrane—killing the parasite.

Breast cancer cells also tend to retain iron. The researchers calculated that if they could

Artemisia is a wormwood plant. Extracts were used in medieval times as a treatment for intestinal worms. More recently, the extract has been combined with alcohol to make a drink called absinthe. Such a beverage cannot be sold in the United States because it is toxic. However, the extract shows promise as a treatment for cancer. (Courtesy of the Agricultural Research Service, U.S. Department of Agriculture)

The green needles and red fruit of the Pacific yew tree are highly poisonous. So is the inner bark, but it is the source of taxol, a medicine that is used to treat cancers. (Courtesy of James Manhart, Texas A&M University)

induce the cancer cells to take up a surplus of iron—made available in the patient's blood by a diet rich in iron—Artemisinin might attack the cancer cells in the same way that it attacked the malaria cells. Laboratory tests in 2004 showed that the drug does kill cancer cells quickly while leaving normal cells unharmed. Further tests are currently underway.

The successful development of these drugs has helped renew the faith of the biomedical research communities that natural materials could be the source of potent medicines. Political support for natural product testing was restored in 1985. By 2003, many thousands of new specimens had been collected and stored in sealed containers at the site of Fort Detrick in Maryland. While most specimens are discarded after preliminary tests show no significant biological activity, over 200 compounds from natural sources have been identified as potentially valuable for drug production.

A Range in Effectiveness

There is a constructive role for medicinal plants in medicine. However, the misuse of these plants could undermine the honorable status of legitimate herbal medicine. For example, the claim that a plant can cure a wide range of ills or relieve inherited diseases such as epilepsy or diabetes is highly suspect.

Potions intended to be curative can be both ineffective and unsafe. Today, scientists know that sassafras oil and a related product, safrol, can cause cancer in laboratory animals.

Extracts from the rosy periwinkle plant provide two chemicals that are important cancer-fighting drugs. (Courtesy of James Manhart, Texas A&M University)

However, some people continue to recommend these materials as home remedies. They are prescribed for colds, fevers, and stomach upsets and are served as a tea brewed from pieces of the root.

Some medicinal claims defy common sense. For example, a tea made from the bracken fern is recommended as a treatment for lung ailments. This fern, which grows in stagnant water, is known to poison grazing cattle. While such a plant poison might be refined into a true medicine, the raw form is unlikely to be beneficial and could kill the unwary.

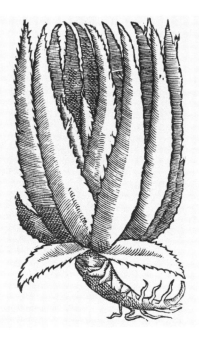

The juice of aloe leaves makes a strong laxative that can weaken a patient. When the juice is used in a skin balm, however, it can relieve itching and redness. (Courtesy of the Photographic Archive Services, National Library of Medicine)

Some traditional herbs are modestly effective. The active ingredient in thistle sap can promote the healing of wounds. Some herbalists also recommend thistle sap to be brewed as a tea. However, the tea is ineffective because the active ingredient is not water soluble.

An extract of *Echinacea,* a cousin to the black-eyed Susan, is useful in enhancing immunities against viral diseases. However, despite claims to the contrary, *Echinacea* is useless in treating tetanus infections or poisonous insect and animal bites.

Raw garlic has some effect against viral infections but not if the smelly but active ingredient, allicin, is removed.

Although most medications are useful for only one illness,

a few can combat more than one. Cortisone, a hormone now made from yams or soybeans, is one of those rare medicines. It is used successfully against arthritis, allergies, skin rashes, and several other medical problems.

Aloe is a plant credited with curing many ailments including both stomach and blood problems. However, if ingested by mouth, aloe acts as a strong and unsafe laxative. The plant is also recommended for many skin problems and is often mixed with cortisone—the proven skin remedy. Used externally, aloe seems to be beneficial.

Today, most folk remedies are not marketed as medicines in the United States. This marketing strategy avoids the requirements imposed by the U.S. Food and Drug Administration on products specifically designated as medicines. Instead, the folk remedies are sold as food products or dietary supplements. Producers of herbal teas, for example, can claim that the teas will bring a wide range of health benefits. However, they are not required to indicate which ingredients have specific medical effects. While they cannot claim that the materials will cure specific diseases, they can use words such as *restorative* that have very general meanings.

5
Vitamins

Originally, vitamins were found only in natural sources—foods made from either animal or vegetable ingredients. Today, synthetic vitamins are found as additives in many foods such as milk, milk products, cereals, and fruit juices—and as pills that supplement the diets of millions of people around the globe. Scientific research has proven that vitamins are essential to health and can cure some diseases. The illnesses cured by vitamins are now known as vitamin deficiency diseases and include maladies such as beriberi, night blindness, pellagra, rickets, and scurvy. These diseases are caused by the inadequate or restricted diets associated with poverty or by the serious food deprivations that accompany a famine. Cultural factors such as a preference for highly refined and processed foods may also provide inadequate or incomplete nourishment and lead to the symptoms of vitamin deficiency. Different groupings of these special chemicals make up the essential vitamins and vitamin complexes—A, B complex, C, and D. Restoring the essential chemicals to the diet—by proper nourishment or by vitamin supplements—relieves the symptoms, and the vitamin deficiency disease is "cured." Only very small amounts of the essential chemicals are required.

The symptoms of a vitamin deficiency were noted in the earliest writings on health care. Egyptian scrolls dating back 3,000 years mention night blindness, a symptom caused by the lack of vitamin A. However, if the ancient Egyptians understood the cause and cure of this condition, such knowledge was lost over time.

During the ensuing millennia, other vitamin deficiency symptoms were included in medical writings and general histories. Usually, such conditions occurred among the poor or downtrodden people in society. The diseases were often taken to be the natural consequences of the poor hygiene and improper or inadequate diets associated with poverty.

By the late 1400s, some scientists, explorers, and physicians began to recognize the importance of diet in maintaining good health and eliminating certain sicknesses. Some of this interest may have resulted from an attempt to aid the poor, but the primary reason was one of financial consideration. Long voyages of exploration were being sponsored by various European governments. The ships were stocked with foods that had to remain more or less edible for long periods of time without the refrigeration or special packaging that is common today. Therefore, after a few days or weeks at sea, fresh fruits and vegetables became rotten or were used up and could not be included in the crew's rations. Weeks or months might pass before a ship came to port or even sighted land and fresh foods could not be replenished. During the times when their diets were restricted, many sailors became ill and often died of a mysterious malady.

Scurvy

More alarms were raised in 1498 when the Portuguese navigator, Vasco da Gama led a squadron of three ships in an attempt to find an ocean route to India and the Spice Islands of the East. After cruising along the west coast of Africa, crew members came ashore near the Cape of Good Hope and sought fresh water and provisions. However, because of a misunderstanding with the local people, the sailors were not allowed to collect fresh supplies. Not long after putting back to sea, crew members began to show symptoms of the mysterious disease. The men suffered loss of appetite, loss of movement, and finally, death. Before reaching the shores of India, 90 sailors had died. A similar episode was experienced by the French explorer, Jacques Cartier, in 1536–37. However, in that instance, most of Cartier's crew members were brought back to health through the ministration of the nearby Native Americans.

Long ocean voyages always brought many hardships, but the onset of this deadly illness was considered catastrophic. Over a short space of time, many sailors could die and the crew would be dangerously shorthanded.

Around 1600, Sir James Lancaster—an adventurous English privateer—sought to solve the problem of scurvy by dietary means. Lancaster had seen dying sailors regain their health after fresh fruits and vegetables were returned to their diets. After careful consideration, he ordered large stores of citrus fruits and ordered his crew members to consume fruit or fruit juice on a regular schedule. During the voyage, far fewer crewmen were stricken with scurvy. Although Lancaster's plan was effective, no one understood why this practice was successful in preventing the onset of the sickness.

CITRUS FRUITS

In 1747, James Lind, a Scottish physician, used his scientific training to determine the reason for Lancaster's success. Lind studied all the available information on the cause, symptoms, and treatment of scurvy. He knew that citrus fruits—especially limes—were thought to prevent or cure the disease. To test the worth of this belief, Lind selected 12 sailors who were suffering from symptoms of scurvy—weakness, bleeding gums, and loose teeth. Lind grouped the men into six pairs. Every day, each pair was given their usual rations plus one other food or drink. One pair received a ration of seawater; another ate a mixture of garlic, mustard, and horseradish; and the third was given spoonfuls of vinegar. The fourth pair drank a quart of cider; the fifth received three doses of an unspecified elixir (a kind of folk medicine); and the last two men were given two oranges and one lemon each day. Four of the groups showed no change in their symptoms. The pair receiving the cider showed a slight improvement, and the sailors receiving the citrus fruit completely recovered. Lind's experiment had proven that citrus fruit could prevent or cure scurvy. Unfortunately, the English Admiralty did not mandate Lind's remedy for about 40 years. After citrus fruit was added to the daily rations of seagoing sailors, the occurrence of scurvy decreased sharply.

The study had several consequences. Lind proved the nutritional benefits of citrus fruits in the treatment of scurvy. More important, Lind's studies were among the first instances of using clinical trials to evaluate a medical treatment. He thereby helped set a standard for all subsequent medical research. Less notably, as the practice of consuming a ration of lime or other citrus juice spread throughout the British navy, foreign observers were prone to adopt the slang term *limey* for English men and women.

Lind's work introduced the study of dietary controls for other health conditions. In the 1870s, researchers with the Japanese Naval Medical Service were able to link the disease beriberi to a dietary insufficiency. A few years later, in the 1880s, medical research established more basic facts about proper nutrition. Scientists concluded that the essential components in all diets included some fats, some carbohydrates provided by sugars or starch, some protein, and small amounts of mineral salt—mainly sodium chloride. By 1900, the vital role of a proper diet was strengthened when scientists determined that rickets, a condition of weakened bones, and pellagra, a disease of the skin and nervous system, could also be controlled by certain foods. Research on such diet-controlled diseases led to the view that there might be other crucial but unidentified "factors" or chemicals found in foods.

Beriberi

Some health-care providers had trouble accepting the idea that a diet that lacked a tiny amount of a mysterious chemical could cause a grave illness. In part, resistance to the idea of a dietary role in disease prevention came about because of the growing influence of the germ theory of disease. Belief in the germ theory had been a struggle for many practical people, but most were finally persuaded in the last quarter of the 19th century. Then, these same people were being asked to acknowledge an even stranger concept about the cause of some diseases. Not everyone was able to accept two mental jolts in such rapid succession.

During the early 1900s, Christiaan Eijkman was experiencing this mental barrier. He was a Dutch physician working in Indonesia who sought the cause of beriberi—a disease rampant in Indonesian cities. Eijkman knew that Japanese research had linked beriberi to diet. However, guided by the germ theory, he thought that some Indonesian foods might contain a disease-causing bacterium. He spent many months at a clinic searching for a microbe in rice kernels, the staple food of the Indonesian people. The microbe was never found. Fortunately, a chance discovery at the clinic led Eijkman to the truth.

This clinic maintained a flock of chickens for local consumption. The chickens were normally fed rough brown rice as their main food. One time, however, the chicken feed supplier failed to make delivery, and the birds were fed the costly white rice intended for the clinic staff and workers. After several days on the white rice diet, the chickens began to show symptoms that looked like beriberi. Eijkman could not fail to notice that the chickens were collapsing and dying in great numbers. He found that the chickens were being fed expensive white rice and ordered a return to their normal, brown rice diet. Soon, the sick chickens returned to health. Eijkman believed that the brown rice played a role in the "cure," but he continued to think that the brown rice hull might contain a specific antidote to an elusive microbe in the rice kernel. Discussions with his colleagues brought out the possibility that the white rice might be missing a key ingredient that was contained in the brown hull. They reasoned that when brown rice is processed—by removing the brown hull—the ensuing product led the unfortunate chickens to die of beriberi. Since the hypothetical microbe was still undetected, the alternative explanation was more plausible. Continued observations showed that Indonesians who restricted their food intake to white rice and little else were prone to succumb to beriberi, while others who ate a varied diet seemed to be immune. Consequently, Eijkman overcame his commitment to the germ hypothesis and published a report that concluded that rice hulls contained a potent substance for the prevention of beriberi. He also cautioned that a diet including only white rice could cause the symptoms of the disease, while a brown rice diet was healthier—and cheaper.

Other research continued while Eijkman was publishing his conclusions. Detailed studies of various nutrients were underway. One research procedure was to feed laboratory animals a diet of highly refined or purified soybeans, yeast, milk, or other protein foods. Animals fed on such foods often failed to thrive and showed symptoms similar to those observed by Eijkman and others during research on dietary diseases. In one study, test animals returned to full health when small amounts of natural, untreated cow's milk were added to their diet. The researchers concluded that untreated milk, a natural rather than a purified food, must contain "small amounts of unknown ingredients that are essential to life." In the early 1920s, similar studies conducted by Frederick Hopkins at

Cambridge University in England led to the idea that natural foods contain tiny quantities of "accessory growth factors." The exact nature of these factors was not known. In spite of the inadequate explanation, the idea was scientifically stimulating, and Eijkman and Hopkins shared the Nobel Prize for Medicine in 1929.

Vitamin B

The chemist who first identified one of these essential ingredients, isolated it chemically, and described its basic molecular structure was the Polish-American scientist, Casimir Funk. Funk was born in Russian-occupied Warsaw, Poland, in 1884. His father was a medical doctor, and his mother was also interested in the field of biology. Casimir was born with a defective hip joint that could not be repaired by surgery. However, this problem did not prevent him from leading a full and active life.

In his early years, Casimir was homeschooled by his parents and tutors. His father was his most influential teacher, and the boy showed an early commitment to a scientific career. When he was about eight years old, he entered a state-sponsored school. Casimir and his parents became dissatisfied with the strong political influence on the curriculum and decided that Casimir's college work should be done in a less political atmosphere. The young scientist was enrolled at a school at Geneva, Switzerland, where his college program was completely focused on the natural sciences. He moved on to a university in Bern, Switzerland, and, in 1904—at the young age of 20—he was awarded an academic doctorate.

Then, as now, young research scientists tend to change jobs frequently, hoping to build a first-class reputation that might lead to a university professorship. Funk began his career in Paris as an assistant biochemist at the Pasteur Institute.

He then moved to Berlin, where he conducted research on proteins and became adept at finding amino acids—the building blocks of proteins— and related chemicals in complicated chemical mixtures.

His one-year appointment at a hospital laboratory in Wiesbaden, Germany, ended as something of a farce. The hospital catered to wealthy patients who came to Wiesbaden to renew their well-being by bathing in the local mineral waters. These waters had gained a far-reaching reputation for their well-advertised— but never scientifically tested— medicinal properties. Funk was hired to analyze the water and conduct clinical studies to establish its health-giving

Casimir Funk in 1927, about the time he moved to Paris, France. (Courtesy of the Library of Congress Photo Archives)

effects. His results indicated that the therapeutic value of the water was very slight. The hospital administrators and all the people who profited from the wealthy patients were distressed by this outcome. Unsurprisingly, Funk was not reappointed when his research contract expired.

After Germany, Casimir traveled to London, where he was offered a position at the Lister Institute. He expected that his research would be focused on the study of hormone functions. However, the director of the Lister Institute, Charles Martin, had developed a strong interest in the disease beriberi because one of his medical school classmates was a British medical officer stationed in South Asia. After Martin's friend had studied the Japanese research that linked beriberi to a dietary deficiency and eliminated other possible culprits, he hypothesized that the disease might be caused by a missing amine. Amines—which belong to a class of small molecules that are carbon-based and contain one or more nitrogen atoms—are found in all plants and animals. On trips back home to London, the colleague discussed his ideas with Martin. When Eijkman's report from Indonesia was published, it strengthened the idea of an amine deficiency and brought the focus of interest to the nature of rice hulls. Martin encouraged Funk to try to isolate the mysterious ingredient.

Funk attacked the problem by using the method of chemical fractionation. Fractionation is a process that begins with the use of a series of different solvents to treat samples of the material being analyzed. In this specific case, the solvents were liquids such as water, alcohol, and various weak acids and were used to dissolve material from finely powdered rice hulls. To begin the experiment, one portion of the powder was steeped in water and a second was steeped in pure alcohol. The respective solvents—water and alcohol—were filtered and evaporated to concentrate the dissolved materials from powdered rice hulls. Each portion was then tested by being fed to animals that were ill from beriberi. The portion that had been steeped in water soon relieved the symptoms but the portion steeped in alcohol did not. This meant that the key ingredient was water-soluble, and the alcohol steeped portion was therefore discarded. The retained residue could now be exposed to other treatments. For example, a portion might be put into a solution of weak acid. A second portion might be exposed to a weak alkali. When the solvents in each portion were filtered and evaporated, the dissolved material could be tested for its influence on the disease. Again, the effective material was retained and the ineffective portion discarded.

Many additional chemical reactions were performed on the water-soluble portion, and Funk finally produced a tiny amount of a pure crystalline substance. He was able to determine that this highly effective beriberi deterrent was in the chemical family of amines. Funk characterized his crystal residue as a vital amine. This led to the composite name, vitamine—eventually shortened to vitamin.

After studying the results of worldwide research, Funk reasoned that there was probably a different vital substance to cure pellagra, rickets, scurvy, and other conditions relieved by dietary changes. Funk's crucial contribution to the health sciences was his determination that certain illnesses could be classified as vitamin deficiency diseases. His ideas meant that a number of diseases could be controlled by methods other than those based on germ theory. Medical research and health-care strategies were broadened to include the study of nutrition and its relationship to disease.

After completing his research program at the Lister Institute, Funk moved to the United States and became an American citizen. He prospered as an industrial chemist until his death in 1967.

When Funk's research findings became widely known, other scientists soon verified his original conjectures. A powerful, fat-soluble, dietary factor was proven to control the symptoms of pellagra. It could be extracted from meat (chiefly from liver) and was also found in fresh vegetables such as carrots. In an attempt to keep the classification orderly, the compound to combat pellagra was given the label "A," while Funk's material to combat beriberi was assigned the label "B." Further studies soon led to the isolation of another water-soluble factor found in the same fresh fruits that prevented scurvy. It was designated as compound "C." Finally, the oil-soluble factor that could control rickets was uncovered and designated vitamin "D."

Practical Nutrition

While the early research on dietary deficiencies was underway, other dramatic events were linked to the vitamin saga. The first decade of the 20th century saw a surge in efforts to explore and map the last of the Earth's geographic frontiers. A major challenge was provided by the new scientific interest in Antarctica. Adventurers such as Englishmen Robert Scott and Ernest Shackleton, Norwegian Roald Amundsen, and others competed to see who could first reach the South Pole and who could first cross the whole Antarctic continent. Supplies of food and other resources were always a problem for the explorers. Early expeditions foundered due to scurvy and, therefore, its prevention was a powerful preoccupation for the later explorers. For example, Roald Amundsen included canned fruit and fruit jams in the expedition's menu as a means to ward off scurvy. Strangely, a major tragedy resulted from too much, rather than too little, vitamin intake.

Vitamin Overdose

In 1911, the young Australian geologist, Douglas Mawson, set out from his home base at the University of Adelaide. He hoped to map the stretch of Antarctic coastline that faced the Australian continent. Mawson, an experienced explorer, had been a member of the Shackleton expedition of 1907–09. Two other talented, experienced trekkers, Belgrave Ninns, an English army officer, and Xavier Mertz, a Swiss mountaineer, made up the exploration party.

Tragedy struck after they had covered about 300 miles of the Antarctic coast. Ninns, guiding the lead sledge, fell through the crust of ice and snow into a deep crevasse. Unfortunately, Ninns lost his life. The two remaining men could not recover Ninns' body or the food and other provisions lashed to his sledge. Mawson and Mertz retraced the path to their home base but soon ran short of food. As had befallen other arctic explorers, they were forced to kill and eat their sled dogs. Since Mertz was unwell, Mawson insisted that Mertz receive the largest share of the raw dog livers. They did not know that the liver of each dog contained 10 times the safe amount of vitamin A. Over several days, the two men consumed the livers of six dogs and both became dangerously ill. Mertz soon died. Mawson was rescued in serious condition, but he survived a malady that no one could explain.

Fortunately, serious vitamin overdose is rare. Water-soluble vitamins, such as the B complexes and vitamin C, are not stored in the body and do not accumulate to lethal levels. High doses of vitamin C, recommended by some to prevent colds or flu, are quickly excreted. Young children rarely receive overdoses of either vitamin A or D, and permanent damage is unlikely. However, moderation in vitamin consumption is strongly suggested because a surplus of vitamins serves no purpose. At worst, kidney functions are stressed as they rid the body of unneeded vitamins.

Vitamin D

As information on vitamins became more widespread, drug and vitamin manufacturers sought ways to profit from the interest in their products. In the 1930s, the connection between vitamin D and bone growth was highly publicized in the popular media. Businesspeople eagerly marketed concentrated vitamin D to the parents of young children who were allegedly susceptible to rickets. One source of concentrated vitamin D was cod liver oil. Many parents in industrialized countries routinely fed their children a tablespoon full of cod liver oil each day. It tasted terrible. To combat this problem, the oil was soon made available in gelatin capsules. The whole movement, however, was out of proportion to the need. When exposed to sunlight, the skin cells of all humans—indeed, all animals—manufacture their own vitamin D. Healthy children who stayed outdoors for even a few minutes a day did not need vitamin D supplements.

While the vitamin D craze was underway, the exact molecular structure of vitamins was being established. Once these structures were known, synthetic versions could be formulated. Mass production made these powerful and low-cost dietary supplements readily available to consumers and led to the practice of adults and children taking a daily dose of all the known vitamins.

There were many consequences to the idea that people need dietary supplements. As scientists searched for other materials to improve health, they established the role of trace minerals. Iron, the first beneficial mineral to be so identified, was followed by the recognition of copper and zinc. People soon began to ingest these additives with their daily dose of vitamins.

Other Nutrients

As nutritional research continued, additional trace factors were discovered. Nutritionists now recognize a total of eight, water-soluble factors found in foods that are rich in vitamin B. These factors make up what is called the "B complex." Other water-soluble substances not included in the B complex group are biotin and inositol. Biotin helps manage energy use at the cellular level and is essential for growth. This vitamin is found in many foods, including organ meat and soy products. Nutritionists are uncertain about the status of inositol. It is a seemingly ordinary sugar-like compound but could have a role in the functioning of nerve cells. Inositol is found in many sources, including beans and nuts. Two new fat-soluble vitamins, E and K, are found in green, leafy vegetables such as broccoli and spinach. Vitamin E protects cells from hazards of all kinds. Vitamin K aids blood-clotting and the storage of calcium.

The terminology for these newly discovered compounds is still somewhat uncertain. For example, one of the new B complex vitamins is called biotin by some nutritionists and vitamin H by others. However, the names of most vitamins are now widely accepted. By the late 1950s, the structures of most vitamins essential to health had been characterized and were available in synthetic form at the corner healthstore.

Prior to the 1930s, few believed that the citizens of industrialized countries needed to supplement their diets. Over a short period of time, vitamins and trace minerals, as well as herbal materials, were added to the daily diets of millions of adults and children around the world. Today, in the United States, the commerce in all types of dietary supplements is a multibillion-dollar business. The popularity of vitamins opened the door to the consumption of many other compounds thought to be related to a person's health or well-being.

6

The Regulation of Medicines

By the late 1700s and early 1800s, many shady business people in the United States were manufacturing health-care products containing medicinal plant materials. Few had credentials in science or medicine. Many successfully promoted their products by presenting dramatic tent shows, staging colorful parades, and placing large advertisements in newspapers.

Their remedies became known as "patent medicines." A patent is legal document that gives the inventor the sole right to produce and sell an invention for a set period of time. In the case of these remedies, the name of the product could be protected by the trademark law. However, the remedy and its formula could not acquire a legally binding patent unless the inventor revealed the ingredients. In those days, few producers wished to disclose their secret mixtures. So, ironically, most early "patent medicines" were not really patented.

The first American patent medicine was marketed in 1796 by a man named Samuel Lee from Connecticut. Like other products of the time, "Lee's Bilious Pills" were advertised as a cure for many different diseases. His pills were supposed to cure yellow fever, jaundice, dysentery, dropsy, worms, and "female complaints" as well as biliousness (heartburn and gas). The name of the product, the only thing protected by the "patent" (really a trademark), was widely advertised. However, the trademark was quickly violated by three other people named Lee. Each marketed his own "Bilious Pills." The three other Lees profited from the advertising financed by original marketer, Samuel Lee.

Members of the medical profession attempted to control or suppress the distribution of patent medicines through their own advertising, public crusades, and lawsuits. The first governmental attempts to curb the marketing of these products began in the late 19th century with laws to correct false or incomplete labeling. The manufacturers were ordered to adhere to the official rules of the professional association of pharmacists. Patent medicine labels had to list both the ingredients and the amount of each ingredient used in the remedy.

These efforts to control patent medicines were countered by some newspaper owners who earned large sums of money for advertising the products. Newspaper proprietors and patent medicine manufacturers were allies because of the financial gains for both.

In those early days, manufacturers of many health-care products made exaggerated and unproven medical claims about their remedies. Thousands bought their products. Even today, people who cannot be helped by conventional medicine sometimes turn to products making unfounded claims and buy questionable remedies. As long as there are difficult or incurable diseases, there will be a market for controversial health-care products.

Other Dangerous Products

While some patent medicines were worthless but harmless, others were dangerous and habit forming. Some of the most important habit-forming drugs come from plants; an example is the opium poppy, a plant native to the Near East. For thousands of years, opium and opium derivatives were considered beneficial for a wide range of medical problems. Abuse of opium derivatives began to draw public attention in the mid-1860s during the latter days of the American Civil War. Morphine, derived from opium, was used for pain relief during and after surgical procedures near the battlefields. Dosages were not controlled, and some patients became heavily dependent on the drug. In many cases, these patients developed a lifelong addiction.

The Food and Drug Administration

The U.S. Food and Drug Administration (FDA), now a part of the Department of Health and Human Services, was established to protect the health of America's citizens. The work of FDA employees is to assess the wholesomeness of all food transported across state boundaries and certify the safety and effectiveness of all prescription drugs.

While these objectives appear to be straightforward, the FDA's responsibility for some types of health products is unclear. The matter of proprietary medicines is one of these areas. Proprietary medicines carry a manufacturer's brand name and are available for sale without a prescription. Most of these products have been on the market for many years. Long-established medicines are not required to pass the tests for safety and effectiveness that are imposed on new drugs. However, the government does require that proprietary drugs be compounded from ingredients that have a long history of use and few, if any, adverse incidents. Aspirin is one of the medicines that the FDA considers to be "generally recognized as safe" (GRAS). This phrase is used by government workers to characterize allowable ingredients. In addition to the GRAS requirement, the names of all the ingredients of all nonprescription drugs must be printed on the label so that consumers will know exactly what they are ingesting.

The field of dietary supplements is another area in which the FDA's involvement is ambiguous. These commercial products include natural ingredients such as herbs. They are considered by their consumers to be health aids and ingested in the form of pills or liquids. Until recently, their legal status was neither food nor medicine, and these products were not subject to food or drug regulations.

Preliminary Efforts

To understand the position of proprietary drugs and dietary supplements in the American culture, it is necessary to look back to the years just before the American Civil War. At that time, people in large cities such as New York became concerned about the unsanitary conditions found in animal slaughterhouses. These were appallingly unclean and the odor of the slaughterhouse districts was dreadful. At about the same time, people began to suspect that the methods used to process foods and drugs might harm consumers. Foods and medicines that were being processed in factories had originally been prepared in family kitchens or by local workers. The factory processes were not as open to the view of consumers. Since the buyers could no longer oversee these activities, they were forced to trust the producers. In many instances, that trust was misplaced. Citizens made their concerns public, and in 1862, President Lincoln appointed Charles M. Wetherill as the first chemist to work in the Department of Agriculture. Although Wetherill's mission was somewhat vague, his presidential appointment was a needed response to citizen complaints.

Wetherill's studies revealed many problems. Meats were adulterated with preservatives that concealed deterioration.

Impure water was used to increase the bulk of milk. Canned goods were contaminated with vermin. Alcohol and other intoxicating ingredients were added to medicines. In 1880, laws governing food adulteration were proposed by Peter Collier, the new chief chemist, but the proposed bill did not pass. Dozens of regulatory laws were introduced during the next 25 years. However, none survived except a provision to inspect imported tea, passed in 1897, and a law governing the quality of vaccines, passed in 1902. That law stated that government controls could be imposed only if a medicine were instantly lethal. Since 1902 to the present, for more than 100 years, political battles have been fought to protect Americans from accidental adulteration and purposeful contamination of foods and drugs. There were few victories.

Most of the fighters were women who had begun to organize themselves into activist groups shortly after the Civil War. The dominant focus for most of these groups was food contamination. However, one of the early militant groups was the Women's Christian Temperance Union. Their concerns about alcohol abuse included the problem of intoxicants in medicines. Manufacturers often added alcohol and narcotics to their proprietary products.

Gradually, various women's organizations began to collaborate on the pure food and drug issue. One such organization was the National Consumers League (NCL). Its initial efforts were directed toward the elimination of child labor. In the late 19th and earl 20th centuries, five- and six-year-old boys and girls worked in factories for about 10 cents a day. Women in the labor movement saw such activities as abusive.

In 1899, the NCL began its campaign for safe medicines. Some historians credit the NCL with providing a political middle ground in which the various women's groups could work together. However, powerful industrial networks opposed all regulations that governed the preparation of foods or the compounding of medicines. Trade associations hired professional lobbyists to influence legislators. Most newspaper publishers opposed the regulation of proprietary medicines because a large proportion of their advertising revenue came from such manufacturers.

During the crucial stages of the struggle for pure food and drug legislation, women did not have the right to vote. Nevertheless, as early as the 1870s, concerted action by organized women, local public health officials, and other interested parties brought reform legislation to individual states. Illinois enacted the earliest pure food laws in 1874 and 1879. During the last two decades of the 19th century, 22 other states enacted similar statues.

Some of these laws were rather ineffective, and the restrictions on proprietary medicines were particularly weak. Enforcement was intermittent for both food and medicine violations. However, the actions of the states provided a good precedent for action at the national level. Elected legislators in many populous states could see that voter opinion—even without the disenfranchised women—favored the regulation of processed foods and medicines.

A public health crisis brought about the first legislative breakthrough at the national level. In 1901, some batches of the vaccine being used to control diphtheria were contaminated. Known as biologics or biologicals, vaccines and antitoxins were typically manufactured locally by city departments of health. The impure vaccine, in this instance, caused an outbreak of tetanus. Five children died in St. Louis, Missouri, after being injected. The problem was not unique. Other children died of the same cause in other cities such as Camden, New Jersey. The spread of the problem across state lines made it a national issue. The U.S. Congress passed the Biologics Control Act in 1902. The responsibility for ensuring purity of such products was handed to the Marine Hospital Service, the main source of health-care personnel at the federal level at that time.

The Muckrakers

At about the same time, weekly and monthly magazines were becoming a source of influence on federal legislators. In the days before radio and television, magazines were a prime source of information and entertainment for relatively well-educated American families. Unlike the cheap tabloid dailies that carried drug ads, *Collier's Weekly* and the *Ladies' Home Journal* were strongly in favor of pure food and drug regulations.

Norman Hapgood, the editor of *Collier's*, developed a deep dislike of medical frauds. He hired a young reporter, Samuel Hopkins Adams, to dig into the proprietary drug situation. In early 1906, his series of 12 articles were republished as a book by the American Medical Association. Almost half a million copies of Adam's exposure of fraudulent drug claims and other scandals were sold at 50 cents each.

Edward Bok, publisher of the *Ladies' Home Journal* in the early 1900s, was another journalist who hired an investigative reporter. His choice was Mark Sullivan, a lawyer turned journalist. Sullivan was successful at uncovering dramatic falsehoods in promotional advertising of proprietary medications. For example, the makers of Lydia Pinkham's Vegetable Compound (a medication designed specifically for women) promised in their promotions that Lydia Pinkham, herself, would personally answer all letters seeking private advice on delicate matters. Sullivan revealed that Pinkham had died more than 20 years before the promise had been made. He proved his accusation with photographs of Lydia Pinkham's gravestone.

Sullivan also exposed an endorsement fraud. For a modest fee, famous people—including national legislators—would allow their names to appear with testimonials about products that they did not use. Other journalists such as Upton Sinclair wrote books about the repulsive practices found in slaughterhouses and food-processing plants. A cluster of such crusading writers became known as "muckrakers." They dramatized the deplorable conditions unearthed in the 1870s by brave and determined women. Many of these conditions still prevailed in the last years of the 19th century.

Research with a Mission

A government scientist named Harvey W. Wiley added more weight to the crusade. He had earned a medical degree from Indiana Medical College in 1871 but never practiced as a physician. For a year after graduation, Wiley taught chemistry at his college and found that his interests lay in teaching and research. He taught at the newly founded Purdue University for several years and then went to Germany to learn the most advanced techniques in analytic chemistry. When Wiley returned to Purdue, officials of the Indiana State Board of Health asked him to conduct research on the sugar products made from the sorghum plant. In 1881, shortly after his research paper was published, he was offered the position of chief chemist at the U.S. Department of Agriculture. The Commissioner of Agriculture hoped to use Wiley's expertise to promote sorghum cultivation as a major source of sugar.

Harvey W. Wiley combined many talents. He was an accomplished chemist, a good manager, a successful showman, and lobbyist. (Courtesy of the National Archives and Research Service)

As the millennium neared, members of Congress were looking for objective information about chemical food preservatives. They were having difficulty reconciling the messages coming from food industry lobbyists with those coming from advocates for stronger federal regulations on food and drugs. As an objective scientist, Harvey Wiley represented a neutral and authoritative position.

By 1902, Wiley conceived a plan to combine his research with a dramatic demonstration. He recruited a score of volunteers from among the young men in his department, the Bureau of Chemistry. The volunteers were fed meals prepared to Wiley's specifications, and the food provided a well-balanced diet. However, the individual items were laced with relatively high amounts of the chemical preservatives used in food-processing plants. Careful records were kept for weeks, and Wiley knew how much chemical adulterant each of the young men had ingested. He also recorded all symptoms of digestive disorders or other malaise. Fortunately, such dangerous research on human subjects would not be allowed today. However, 100 years ago, Wiley's so-called Poison Squad received positive publicity across the country. Citizens paid rapt attention to the idea that their family members might be consuming poison with their meals.

Wiley was more than a showman of science. He made a serious effort to obtain agreements between diverse groups such as the leaders of the commercial drug industry and the leaders of the reform movements. The National Consumers League was actively backing Wiley at this time. With such help, he was able to convince President Theodore Roosevelt and members of Congress that they would lose few supporters if they adopted his suggestions for legislation. The Pure Food and Drug Act became law in 1906 and went into effect on January 1, 1907.

Regulations

The new law provided for two parallel programs: a scientific research function and a law enforcement function. Both programs were invested in the Bureau of Chemistry, a division of the Department of Agriculture. As bureau chief, Wiley continued as head of scientific research, and he appointed a young attorney, Walter Campbell, to lead the enforcement staff. Although the future looked promising, a number of problems remained.

Wiley and Campbell were soon aware of the weaknesses in the new legislation. Some sections of the new law were too vague to demand strict obedience. Others, such as the requirement of a case-by-case basis for the prohibition on harmful food additives, slowed down any positive steps to improve food safety. For example, Wiley wanted to prohibit the use of sodium benzoate—a questionable additive—as a food preservative. A member of the New York house of representatives who was part owner of a food-canning company opposed this action. The representative took his case directly to President Theodore Roosevelt. The president invited Wiley and his boss, the Secretary of Agriculture to meet with the representative in the president's office. All went well for Wiley until the president inquired about Wiley's views on saccharin, an artificial sweetener made from coal tar. Wiley said that he opposed its use as an additive in canned corn. Since Roosevelt used saccharin daily on the advice of his personal physician, he thought of saccharin as a boon. Wiley's whole position as an advocate of regulation was undermined. The president denied the prohibition of sodium benzoate because of Wiley's negative comments about saccharin. Presidential whims rather than science sometimes determined the fate of food additives.

In any case, the president signed the Pure Food and Drug Law. The main provisions of the new law concerned truthful labeling. Makers could claim many medical effects—even cures for specific diseases—with no restrictions as long as the label listed all the ingredients. In 1912, Congress attempted to change the law to cover false claims but could not agree on the proper wording. Occasionally, some makers were forced to pay fines for false claims, but the amount of the fine was usually a small fraction of the profits from the product. The most important consequence of the 1906 law was to help suppress the practice of including narcotics and large amounts of alcohol in proprietary medicines.

Clearly, the simple passage of a new law did not remove the political opposition to the regulation of drugs and food additives. Public outrage had led to the passage, but many legislators privately held negative attitudes toward the law. Indeed, Congress gave the Chemistry Bureau an inadequate budget that failed to allow for the proper management of the new agency. Only minor structural changes in the bureau were possible, such as the 1927 ruling to separate the departments of research and law enforcement. The research function remained with the Bureau of Chemistry, and in 1930, the enforcement branch was renamed the Food and Drug Administration.

By the 1930s, enlightened leaders in the field of medicinal drugs recognized that government standards helped to keep their business fair and competitive, and they began backing some of the newly proposed amendments to the law. Then, great public furor caused by a deadly mistake in 1937 added to the clamor for tighter controls. A small drug company distributed a medicine that promptly killed 107 people, including many children. The company had sought to produce an easy-to-swallow medicine containing the antibiotic sulfanilamide. Since sulfanilamide is oily and only slightly soluble in water, an organic solvent for oily compounds was needed. The chosen solvent was propylene glycol, a safe, common food additive. Production line workers mistakenly used a chemical called diethylene glycol, a highly poisonous substance. The drug was recalled by the manufacturer but not before the deaths had occurred. No one could explain the presence of the poisonous diethylene glycol in a factory that produced medicines.

A carefully rewritten law, the Federal Food, Drug and Cosmetics Act, was passed in 1938. It required that proof of safety must be established before a drug could be sold to consumers. Along with other provisions, this law also established the procedures whereby a physician must prepare a written prescription to allow a pharmacist to dispense a drug.

In 1940, the FDA was transferred from the Department of Agriculture to a new bureaucracy called the Federal Security Agency (predecessor to the Social Security Administration). Walter Campbell, who had been Wiley's enforcement agent, was named commissioner and further changes were made in the organization. Late in the year, the basic law was amended again so that the requirement for a doctor's prescription in the dispensing of drugs was strengthened.

Leaders in the FDA sensed the need to work more closely with the general public, and in 1952, they created a department that was more responsive to consumer needs. The amended law and other innovations temporarily quieted the advocates for stronger and more inclusive laws. However, a grave problem soon became apparent in Europe.

Drug Issues

In 1960, German chemists developed a drug to be used as a tranquilizer. In addition to its main purpose, the drug, thalidomide, proved helpful in preventing the stomach upsets that are common in early pregnancy. Because of this, doctors and pharmacologists realized that the drug must have a direct effect on the patient's nervous system. However, physicians considered this finding to be a beneficial result of taking the new drug.

Thalidomide was a great success in Germany and Great Britain. The producer began to anticipate a large American market and sent sample materials to the company's U.S. sales representatives. The salespeople were encouraged to distribute the drug to physicians as a way to carry out informal field trials. At that time, such actions were within the law because the U.S. government allowed the importation of drugs that had been approved by trustworthy countries. However, one FDA staff member was worried about thalidomide. She knew that drugs with strong effects on the central nervous system could be passed through the biological barriers that normally protect the unborn child. No one in Europe had examined the possible consequences of such exposure. She began to raise questions. Soon, reports from Europe told of an outbreak of malformed babies. Careful checks revealed that the mothers of these babies had taken thalidomide during the early months of their pregnancies. Aware of the scientist's warnings, the FDA quickly recalled the drug and few cases of the condition occurred in the United States. However, as time progressed, dozens of cases were identified in Europe, and people were appalled by the harm done to infants and their families. Media sources on both sides of the Atlantic circulated heartbreaking stories of the malformed babies.

After the terrifying thalidomide affair, the U.S. Congress passed further amendments to the basic law. The new legislation required that proof of a drug's effectiveness and safety must be established before the drug could be dispensed by anyone—including medical practitioners. In 1968, a backup study was conducted under the guidance of the National Academy of Sciences to review the effectiveness of drugs that had been released for use in prior years. The academy's panel rejected many of the old drugs because their effectiveness had never been proved.

Although the safeguards for medicines had been strengthened, FDA officials became more intent on providing understandable and meaningful medical information to everyone. They realized that more people—most with little medical knowledge—were acting as their own health-care providers. They also understood that those who received prescriptions from their physicians might not follow the orders for taking the medicine.

Information Issues

As FDA officials became increasingly concerned about the misuse of prescription drugs, they decided to require that drug companies prepare information about their products. The required information was a detailed list of the ingredients, uses, recommended dose schedules, and side effects of each drug. Although FDA officials were able to inform most doctors of this new ruling by standard "Dear Colleague" letters, they had no budget to reach the general public. Therefore, the drug companies were required to include the information with every container of medicine. The companies were unenthusiastic about this maneuver because they believed that listing the possible side effects would frighten their customers. For a time, drug companies were allowed to place such information on the labels of prescription medicines. However, the type on the labels tended to be very small and the information too long and difficult to understand.

The practice of using inserts became common in the mid-1970s. Such inserts are pieces of paper printed with the required drug information and folded to fit into each box or bag containing a prescription medicine. This method of information distribution was begun when the FDA questioned the safety of the artificial sweetener saccharin. Saccharin was the sugar substitute preferred by many people who were on self-imposed or physician-imposed diets. These advocates—and the companies that manufactured and distributed the product—made their displeasure known to members of Congress.

Although FDA officials wanted to ban its use, they were unable to so. However, each bottle of saccharin was required to have a warning on the label and a warning insert included in the packaging.

The HIV epidemic was the main medical crisis of the 1980s. At first, there were no real treatments for the lethal AIDS virus, and the medical profession was stymied. Indeed, there were no drugs to offer relief from the symptoms and discomfort of the drawn-out terminal phase. At about the same time that the AIDS crisis became apparent, the FDA had achieved some success in passing laws to assure the safety and effectiveness of medicines. Lengthy tests and trials were required before a drug would be approved. HIV victims regarded these new requirements as unnecessary retardants to the development and approval of new drugs for their disease. AIDS victims, those at risk of infection, and their supporters were angered by these delays and staged many public protests. Among the most effective was a demonstration at the FDA headquarters in Rockville, Maryland, that attracted much press and TV coverage.

Even before the public displays, FDA officials had been seeking ways to speed the drug review and approval process. They needed the backing of Congress and the top officials in the Department of Health and Human Services to modernize the review procedures and secure the funding to increase the staff. Support was ultimately provided. The HIV crisis is a prime example of how concerned citizens can influence the government in the areas of scientific and medical policies.

At the present time, FDA officials are rethinking their concerns about dietary supplements. Citizen groups—both for and against the testing of these health aids—have grown more vocal as marketers have increased their use of the Internet and posted unsubstantiated therapeutic claims for their products.

The Federal Trade Commission (FTC) has the prime responsibility to spot such an advertisement. FDA and the

FTC personnel have joined in an agency task force to ensure truth in advertising of medical supplements. If a violation is found, the marketer is sent a letter to warn that curative claims indicate their product is a medicinal drug—not just a food supplement.

Although dietary supplements do not require proof of effectiveness and safety, medicinal drugs are held to a higher standard. Therefore, the packager must either drop the claims of medical effects or submit the product for testing by qualified scientists. Failure to comply with the warning may mean confiscation of the product and/or criminal charges for the manufacturer. The enforcement agents are typically U.S. Marshals and are directed by court orders that are requested by the regulators.

Criminal charges have rarely been the outcome of a failure to comply. However, a series of problems has forced FDA officials to become more aggressive in enforcing the law. In 1989, a large quantity of a dietary supplement known as l-tryptophan was imported from Japan, repackaged by American distributors, and marketed by health-food stores. This substance is a natural amino acid but is not considered essential to human nutrition. It is typically produced by bacterial fermentation, a process similar to the production of cheese.

In early 1990, the Centers for Disease Control and Prevention in Atlanta, Georgia, recorded more than 1,000 cases of a rare disease called eosinophilia-myalgia syndrome, or EMS. Nine deaths were reported from the disease. The public health officers linked the outbreak of EMS to the consumption of the l-tryptophan that had been imported from Japan the previous year. Although it was unclear whether the disease resulted from the l-tryptophan itself or from some contaminant in the fermentation process, prudence dictated that the shipment be recalled. It is still not known whether the l-tryptophan was the direct cause of the disease but follow-up studies revealed that the possible contaminant was detected in samples of l-tryptophan collected from unrelated sources. Regardless of the outcome of this case, l-tryptophan should not be offered for sale in the United States since it has never been classified as an acceptable dietary supplement.

In February 2000, the FDA issued a medical advisory to health-care professionals that the dietary supplement Saint-John's-wort could impair the action of a drug used to treat HIV patients. Saint-John's-wort had been tested in clinical trials as an antidepressant, and the result revealed that the substance works as well as the more conventional drugs with which it was compared. However, because of its apparent interaction with other drugs, the advisory letter suggested that care providers question their HIV patients about the use of dietary supplements.

Exactly two years later, the FDA sent a warning letter to all firms that offer ephedra compounds for sale via the Internet. Clinical studies funded by the National Institutes of Health had revealed that the ingestion of compounds containing ephedra led to serious health risks—such as problems with the circulatory system. These risks were most prevalent in young men who were seeking to lose weight or gain muscle mass while preparing to appear in strenuous athletic events. The study found no particular benefits from the use of these compounds. In other words, neither the desired suppression of appetite nor the change in metabolism actually resulted from the ingestion of ephedra. The net outcome was serious risk with no gain. In 2004, the FDA banned the use of ephedra materials in dietary supplements.

These and other disturbing episodes have increased the likelihood of reforms in U.S. laws governing the compounding and marketing of dietary supplements.

7

South American Expeditions

South America contains some of the world's most extensive rain forests, which have provided humans with several important medicines. Some of this astonishing variety of plant life has been tested for medicinal properties, but many plants remain to be investigated. Today, scientists and environmentalists are fighting to preserve the forests from eradication by commercial interests. Many scientists fear that untested plant species will be destroyed before they can be analyzed. It is hoped new wonder drugs may be found among those unstudied plants.

Early History of Spanish America

In 1498, Christopher Columbus completed his third voyage to the Americas. He landed near the mouth of the Orinoco River in present-day Venezuela. Columbus's journeys had been financed by the Spanish monarchs, Ferdinand and Isabella, and Spain soon led the world in both exploration and colonization. During the next 10 years, Spaniards explored the east coast of South America. In 1513, the Spanish captain Vasco de Balboa trekked across the narrow Isthmus of Panama. He was the first European to stand on the eastern shore of the Pacific Ocean.

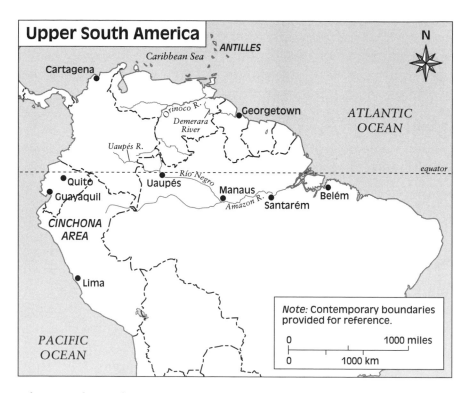

The map shows the major cities and rivers of the north-central area of South America. The cities served as supply bases and resting places for explorers. The rivers served as their passageways.

In 1527, another Spanish captain, Ferdinand Magellan, entered the Pacific by sailing around the southern tip of South America. Francisco Pizarro duplicated that route to the Pacific and in 1535 established the city of Lima, in modern-day Peru. Other Spaniards settled at Cartagena on the Caribbean coast in what is now Colombia. Their countrymen also occupied Quito, a city previously held by the Inca in a high Andean valley near the equator. Today it is in Ecuador.

In pre-Columbian times, the Inca people lived along the Pacific coast and in the central regions of the Andes Mountains.

The highly developed Inca civilization occupied an area with many gold and silver mines. The Spanish invaders saw evidence of these riches in the Incas' artifacts—their statues, jewelry, and other objects made of gold and silver. In their quest for wealth and power, the Spanish seized the artifacts, exploited the mines, enslaved the Inca, and helped destroy the already declining Inca civilization. Attracted by stories of fabulous wealth, Europeans explored the mountainous portions of South America for the next three hundred years.

To ensure a steady flow of precious metals into Spain, the Spanish monarchs retained control over the richest areas of the continent.

Open-Air Science

Some Spanish and Portuguese explorers had a modest interest in science and recognized that the New World should be studied as well as exploited. However, the financing of research expeditions was given a very low priority by European rulers. These limited resources were partly responsible for the lack of scientific exploration in South America. Other factors, too, slowed the study of the continent's plant and animal life.

Few Europeans were trained as scientists in the time of Columbus. Indeed, there was no clear definition of science or of careers in which scientific knowledge or research played a major role. Some members of the government, the military, and the religious orders were interested in investigating the world around them. This interest, however, was not their main work. Few individuals possessed both the interest and the independent income to allow them to make scientific investigation a full-time occupation. Therefore, in the years between the early 1500s and the 1900s, a relatively small number of individuals were able to investigate the scientific riches of South America.

During that long stretch of time, the people who were able to do such research were known as naturalists. This title meant that the individual had a working knowledge of astronomy, geology, geography, zoology, and botany. Their formal education was often in the field of medicine or the study of philosophy with an emphasis on mathematics. The knowledge and skill required to conduct scientific research was often self taught.

Although some of the individuals who came to South America were concerned with finding medicinal plants, most were interested in discovering new and unusual ornamental plants to beautify the gardens of Spain and Portugal. Most Europeans believed that they had located and perfected all the important sources of medicine. The specific search for medicinal plants in South America is a relatively recent enterprise.

Prior to the late 20th century, expeditions to South America had much broader scientific goals. The early discoveries of medicinal plants in South America were often accidental. Today, the search for medicinal plants combines anthropology and botany. This field is called ethnobotany.

In spite of the informal way in which early explorers sought medicinal plants, Europeans found some useful specimens in South America. Three explorers were responsible for opening the continent to the later scientists who focused on locating medicinal plants.

Charles-Marie de La Condamine, Immortal of France

Although preceded by a few Spanish naturalists, Charles-Marie de La Condamine of France was the first serious scholar to gain a broad scientific perspective on South America. La Condamine was born in 1701, the son of a high official in the court of the French king Louis XIV. When he was 18, he finished his formal training in mathematics and joined the French army as a junior officer. Ironically, his first active duty was fighting against the Spanish. Between battles, La Condamine conversed with a captured Spanish soldier who had served with the Spanish forces in Peru. The descriptions of the Andes, the South American rivers, and the cities of the Inca fired La Condamines's imagination.

At the age of 29, La Condamine was elected to the French Academy of Sciences. In 1730, shortly after his election, the academy was plagued by a controversy between followers of Isaac Newton, an English mathematician, and Jacques Cassini, an Italian-French scientist. Newton had theorized that the Earth was slightly flattened at the North and South Poles because of its rotation and the effects of the Moon's gravity. In contrast, Cassini proposed that the Earth was slightly elongated toward the Poles. The opposing sides conducted great verbal battles within the walls of the academy. French patriots favored Cassini's ideas because he had French family connections. However, academy members finally realized that the issue was vital to the future of ocean travel and too important to be resolved by debate—they needed evidence.

All the members knew that sailors must be supplied with reliable astronomical measurements in order to navigate their ships across the oceans. The academy began making plans to gain this information. To be absolutely accurate, the measurements had to be made as close as possible to the equator and the North Pole. Within a short time, the northern base was set up in Lapland near the Arctic Circle.

The French soon discovered that finding a good equatorial site was not as easy. Although huge areas of both Africa and South America are crossed by the equator, gaining access to the best possible sites presented formidable problems. The African coast was guarded by pirates who would not allow the scientific expedition to land. In South America, Quito, a city in the Andes, was an ideal location to make the celestial observations. But Quito was controlled by Spain—a former enemy of France. Nevertheless, negotiations were begun and King Philip of Spain agreed to permit the expedition. The necessary royal commands were signed and the leaders of the French Academy began to organize the expedition to South America. They needed a young, brave, and vigorous scientist to lead the party. They selected La Condamine.

The expedition team consisted of 10 members, including Joseph de Jussieu, an expert in botany. In November 1735, the group landed in the seaport of Cartagena. They were joined by two Spanish naval officers, their escorts for the rest of the trip. Today, Cartagena, a city in northwestern Colombia, would seem an awkward beginning for a trip to Quito, the capital of Ecuador. Then, Cartegena was the official gateway to the Spanish territories. This isolated location was designed to keep people unacceptable to Spain out of Spanish lands.

La Condamine's expedition crossed the Isthmus of Panama and headed south for the coastal town of Guayaquil, several hundred miles from Quito. The group was met in Guayaquil by a local leader, Pedro Maldonado. Maldonado wanted to act as guide to the prestigious group of scientists and told them of his new route to Quito. La Condamine was worried about his men traveling on an untried route and ordered them to use the established way. He alone accompanied Maldonado on the new route.

His route proved rewarding. When La Condamine and Maldonado reached the foothills of the Andes, they were met by natives who showed La Condamine a material made from the sap of a tree. The material, called caoutchouc, was a stretchy clothlike substance. Today, caoutchouc is known as rubber. While not a medicine, rubber has come to play a major role in health care. It has been used for surgical gloves, rubber sheets, tires on movable stretchers, and countless other important objects. Indeed, La Condamine saw an immediate use for the material. He wrapped his scientific instruments in the material to keep them from breaking and then made a container to protect them from the frequent rain. When the Frenchman returned home, he informed his colleagues about this useful plant product. La Condamine is regarded as the modern European discoverer of rubber.

La Condamine and the other members of his expedition were reunited at Quito and soon the group began to survey a 200-mile (320-km) strip of land. This strip would serve as a baseline in their mathematical calculations to determine the size of the Earth at the equator. The process took a full year.

By measuring the angle of a certain star from each end of the baseline, the scientists determined that Newton's theory was correct. The expedition to the Arctic Circle had already confirmed Newton's position. The mission had been accomplished, and the men were ready to return home. La Condamine, however, was not finished with his explorations of South America. He decided to travel down the eastern slopes of the Andes and then navigate the Amazon River to the Atlantic coast. La Condamine's journey down the Amazon River helped to reveal the vast resources of the rain forests. European residents along the 2,000 miles (3,200 km) of the upper Amazon were mainly Jesuit missionaries sent to convert the natives to Christianity.

The bark of the rubber tree is cut into at an angle so that the sap, called latex, will flow down into the cup attached to the trunk. (Courtesy of Scott Gasch)

These missionaries were able to help La Condamine and others survive the rigors of the Amazon region.

Indeed, a local Jesuit priest helped La Condamine enter the river near its highest navigable point in the eastern foothills of the Andes. Other Jesuits along the Amazon told the French explorer about various useful plants that grew in the area. They described quinine and its ability to reduce fevers. They also related the paralyzing and deadly effects of curare and how native fisherman used extracts from the barbasco plant to intoxicate fish. Maldonado and La Condamine are credited with opening up the Amazon River area.

La Condamine recognized the great importance of four South American plants. When he returned to Europe, La Condamine took back samples of rubber and information about harvesting and processing the useful, stretchy material. He carried back seeds and seedlings of the cinchona tree and hoped to cultivate the tree that alleviated malaria. After his return to France, La Condamine experimented with curare and was the first European to note that its effects were not necessarily fatal. He also collected specimens of the barbasco plant, the juice of which was used by natives to intoxicate fish and make them easy to capture. This plant produces saponins, a type of chemical used as a raw material in many medicines. Much later, it was found that rotenone, an extract of the barbasco, is an effective natural insecticide.

Fusée Aublet

Another French scientist, Fusée Aublet, sailed for South America about 20 years after La Condamine completed his explorations and returned to Europe. Unfortunately, Aublet's life is not as well documented as that of his countryman. Nevertheless, some modern botanists regard Aublet as the founder of ethnobotany. An ethnobotanist obtains information about new plants by consulting with native peoples and records how their local plants are used for food, medicine, clothing, and shelter. Aublet was the first scientist to use this approach.

As a young man, Aublet may have been schooled in medicine as well as botany. He served as a druggist's apprentice in Spain and, briefly, as a medical assistant in the Spanish army. After his army service, Aublet accepted a position as a druggist at the Charity Hospital in Paris, France. He then gained employment with the Company of the Indies, a French colonizing and trading organization. The young scientist was assigned to their base on Mauritius, a large island that lies off the east coast of Africa. Aublet worked on Mauritius as a dispenser of medicinal herbs during the 1750s and early 1760s.

At that time, the French government controlled a territory on the upper east coast of South America that came to be called French Guiana. Fusée Aublet was chosen to inventory the medicinal plants of that area. He arrived at the French territory in 1762 and completed his work in 1764. He collected and identified many new species of plants including 124 with medicinal or nutritional uses.

Alexander von Humboldt, Liberal Aristocrat

The next extraordinary European explorer of South America arrived on that continent in 1799. This German scientist, Alexander von Humboldt, was born in 1769. He was among those lucky individuals whose family wealth allowed him to be a full-time naturalist. His father died when he was 10 years old and his mother, Marie Elisabeth von Holwede, took responsibility for his education. She had high ambitions for her sons' careers. Marie Elisabeth carefully selected the tutors who were retained to teach Alexander and his older brother, Wilhelm. After leaving home at age 16, his education continued at military schools, and he gained his training as a scientific explorer at German universities. His interest in the arts, languages, and science was due in part to his mother's continuing influence.

After Napoleon's invasion of Egypt, Humboldt, then in his late 20s, was invited to join a French expedition to that country. The proposed journey did not take place because the English fleet defeated Napoleon's forces and blockaded Egypt. After this change of plans, Humboldt and Aimé Bonpland, a botanist who had planned to go to Egypt with him, decided to become partners in research projects. This partnership proved fruitful.

After their hopes to explore Egypt and North Africa were frustrated by the political situation, Humboldt and Bonpland decided to explore South America. Since Spain still controlled access to South America, permission to travel there was required. Humboldt's family connections assured them an audience with the Spanish king Charles IV. Happily, the two scientists received a special passport from the king that secured complete cooperation from the Spanish officials in South America. After careful preparations and interviews with Spaniards who had been to South America, the

This statue was erected in Berlin, Germany, in honor of Alexander von Humboldt. (Courtesy of Galen Frysinger)

two left Spain in the spring of 1799. A few months later, they arrived in Venezuela at the mouth of the Orinoco River.

The explorers were eager to confirm the truth of a rumor that La Condamine had carried to Europe. The earlier explorer had been told that there was a natural canal that connected the Orinoco and the Amazon Rivers. Humboldt and Bonpland wanted to locate this connection if it existed. Because rivers were the principal means of transportation through the continent, a connection between the two important waterways could have major economic consequences.

Humboldt and Bonpland traveled first on the Río Apure, a tributary of the Orinoco River. They sailed down the Apure, entered the Orinoco well above its mouth, and then turned upstream on the main river. After many difficulties, they arrived at a plateau in the Venezuelan highlands where the Orinoco divides into slow-moving streams, one of which turns away from the others and flows into the Río Guiana. The Guiana joins the Río Negro, a large tributary of the Amazon. Thus, Humboldt did find a connection between the Orinoco and the Amazon. Sadly, it was not navigable. Instead, it was a shallow, slow-moving creek.

During their river travels, Bonpland had been busy collecting both ornamental and medicinal plant specimens. After confirming the truth of La Condamine's story, the explorers decided to trek to the Río Negro, sail down to the Amazon, and then continue along its course. Bonpland sent his plant collection down the Orinoco with some native messengers and the pair set off overland to the Río Negro.

Much of their route was through Brazil, then under Portuguese rule. The passport endorsed by the king of Spain was no longer valid. In fact, the explorers were promptly arrested as spies when they reached the first military base on the Amazon. It took some time to untangle the confusion. During their return to Venezuela, Bonpland contracted malaria. He was saved from death by large quantities of locally produced quinine.

After some side trips, the pair continued their explorations along the west coast. They sailed up the Río Magdalena to Bogotá, the capital of New Granada (now Colombia). In Bogotá, they met with José Mutis, a remarkable man who combined the talents of physician, priest, and botanist. The two European scientists had studied Mutis's collection of plant specimens in Madrid, Spain, before leaving Europe for South America.

While in the western area of South America, Humboldt began a series of studies that concerned both geography and botany. He focused on climatic variations and the relationship between plants and the temperature and altitude in which they grow. Such studies allowed Humboldt to explain why plants from low-lying areas of cool regions have strong similarities with plants that thrive at high elevations near the equator. This observation was important for those who would later attempt to domesticate medicinal plants.

Bonpland was particularly interested in collecting plant specimens from a certain area around Loja in Chile. According to legend, quinine from trees in this vicinity allegedly cured Countess Chinchón, a member of the Spanish nobility, in 1638. Her family name was later given to the cinchona (chinchon) tree from which quinine is derived.

While in the area, Humboldt observed the harvesting practices used to remove bark from the wild cinchona trees. He became concerned, as had La Condamine, that the practice would kill the trees and the species would become extinct, eliminating the source of natural quinine forever. Their concerns mirror those of late 20th-century scientists who were worried about the survival of the Pacific yew, a source of taxol.

The explorers chose a coastal route for their journey from Colombia to Chile. Humboldt wondered why the long stretch through Chile and Peru was so arid compared to the coast of Colombia. His knowledge of geophysics provided the answer.

The sea off the coast of Chile and Peru is remarkably cold, but the coastal lands are warm. When the cold, moisture-laden winds blow from the ocean, the heat from the land warms the breezes and increases their capacity to carry moisture. Consequently, the air holds the moisture until forced to rise by the Andes Mountains, which lay some distance from the coast. Later, in recognition of Humboldt's activities, the coastal current of cold water, 150 miles (240 km) wide and 1,000 miles (1,600 km) long, was named the Humboldt Current. This stream of water is recognized as the controlling factor in the rich fishing grounds off the coasts of Peru and Chile.

After he returned to Europe, Humboldt was credited with the "rediscovery of South America" and his adventures generated great curiosity about the continent. Shortly after Humboldt returned home, the peoples of South America overthrew their Spanish and Portuguese colonizers. The leaders of the newly independent countries were far more hospitable to scientific expeditions than the European kings had been.

Richard Spruce, Yorkshireman

Richard Spruce was born in 1817 in Gansthorpe, a village in Yorkshire, England. His mother died soon after he was born. Spruce's father, a schoolteacher, remarried a few years later. The new young wife gave birth to a succession of daughters and Dick's father and stepmother were busy with their growing family. Young Dick found himself free from parental supervision at a relatively early age. Fortunately, he was a bright boy and after completing school in the village he arranged for his own further education. For example, Spruce persuaded the local physician to tutor him in Latin and Greek.

On his own, Spruce gathered interesting plants from the moorland around the village and spent much time identifying and classifying his collection. By the age of 20, he had enlarged his collection to include 485 flowering species. Some of his rare finds were later included in catalogs of British plants.

Spruce followed in his father's footsteps and became a teacher at a college preparatory school. Although he did not teach botany, he spent his free time learning about that science. Spruce read many books on the subject and discussed his ideas with other amateur scientists.

Spruce also read accounts of South American expeditions and yearned to investigate plant life on that continent. After a year of teaching, Spruce realized that he did not enjoy the profession. However, he was virtually penniless and could not hope to find the resources to explore the New World. Spruce continued to teach and pursued his botanical studies as a sideline. Fortunately, his independent studies were carefully documented and his observations were accepted for publication in the scientific journals of the day. Spruce soon gained a good reputation among established scientists.

In 1844, Spruce's school went out of business and he needed to find another job. To further his interest in botany, Spruce had begun exchanging letters with Sir William Hooker. Hooker was associated with the British government's Botanical Gardens at Kew in suburban London. The older scientist unsuccessfully attempted to obtain a curatorship for Spruce at a museum in one or another of the British colonies. Hooker then introduced Spruce to George Bentham, a professional plant collector. Bentham had just returned from a successful plant-finding expedition in Spain and employed Spruce as an independent subcontractor. Bentham paid for Spruce to conduct an expedition to Spain. He also agreed to act as Spruce's agent in the sale of botanical specimens to museums and herbariums across Europe. The two-year enterprise was successful and they discussed an expedition to South America.

Two British naturalists, Alfred Wallace and Henry Bates, were already in South America surveying insects, birds, and animals. Spruce carefully read reports that the naturalists had sent back to England. He realized that his knowledge of botany would increase the depth of the investigations. The plans were completed for Spruce to join Wallace and Bates in South America. At last, he would realize his dream of exploring the new continent.

Spruce's ship departed from Liverpool in the early summer of 1849. It docked at Belém, Brazil, at the mouth of the Amazon River. As soon as he had rested from his trip, the young scientist began to collect exotic plants.

Although a few earlier Amazon explorers had some background in the study of botany, Spruce was the first to have the necessary knowledge, experience, and skills to undertake a thorough investigation of plant life in the area. After spending three months in Belém learning Portuguese and studying the local plants, Spruce embarked by sailboat for Santarém, about 500 miles (800 km) up the Amazon. The steady trade winds off the Atlantic pushed the boat against the river current.

Spruce collected plants whenever the boat came to shore. Along the way, he found a vine called sarsaparilla, which later became popular as a tonic and flavoring agent. Sarsaparilla is closely related to the Chinese plant that Rauwolf had found at Aleppo when he toured the Near East in the 1570s.

When Spruce reached Santarém, he met with Alfred Wallace and Henry Bates. Bates was in the process of collecting and identifying some 14,000 species of insects—8,000 of which were new to European scientists.

While staying in Santarém, the three English scientists experienced an unusually harsh rainy season. The downpour raised the water level by 40 feet (12 m) and the lands along the Amazon were flooded for hundreds of miles. The floods caused some dormant plants to bloom and Spruce was able to study these seldom-seen species. He spent a year in Santarém investigating the local plants.

Rubber trees were plentiful in the region and Spruce carefully recorded his observations of the harvesting of rubber. He

Extracts from the roots of sarsaparilla have been used to treat many diseases and were once a popular ingredient in carbonated beverages. (Courtesy of Alice Tangerini and the Smithsonian Institution)

noted that the native workers slashed the tree bark in several places and allowed the sap to flow into cups attached under the cuts. The sap of the tree was the raw material for making rubber.

From time to time, Spruce sent his botanical specimens back to Europe. His work was praised and more and more museums wanted his collections. By this time, Spruce had collected thousands of species and new ones were being added every day.

After Spruce left Santarém, he established a base at Manaus. His next venture was to travel up the Río Negro. During a stop in São Gabriel, a small village well upriver from Manaus, Spruce received a disturbing message. Wallace had contracted malaria and was near death. Spruce hastened to his friend's side and helped nurse him back to health.

After Wallace recovered, Spruce set out for the far upper reaches of the Río Uaupés. He again traveled by canoe and was forced to make frequent portages around the rapids and waterfalls. While on this journey, Spruce was introduced to a potent drug derived from a plant. During a religious ceremony, he drank a potion the natives called *caapi*. Fortunately, he did not have to drink second cup. If so, Spruce would have experienced the hallucinations that the native Indians sought for themselves. Spruce recognized that this mind-bending plant material might have beneficial properties when used as a medicine. He reasoned that if the native population regarded the substance as potent, it was worth further investigation.

Spruce believed that native traditions were often valid and therefore important to his work. He studied the native languages and asked many questions about the local plants. Spruce recorded the native names, uses, and medicinal properties of the plants that he classified. His work was much more comprehensive than that of Aublet. Consequently, he is regarded by more scientists as the father of ethnobotany—the study of the relationship between native cultures and local plants.

Spruce sent the specialists at Kew Gardens samples and information about medicinal plants. Unfortunately, some cuttings—including the roots of the vine used to make *caapi*—spoiled before they reached England. A later sample of the vine was tested and revealed an alkaloid, a type of bitter enzyme that can induce hallucinations. Because enzymes have important medicinal properties, Spruce had been correct in his assessment of the plant. He listened ever more carefully when natives discussed the "magic powers" of local plants.

Spruce spent several more months collecting plants along the upper Orinoco and its tributaries. He was finally worn down by bouts of malaria, and in 1854 spent months near the town of San Fernando, Venezuela, recovering from the disease. When his health improved, Spruce headed back down the Río Negro to Brazil. When he reached Manaus, he found that the town was enjoying a booming economy in rubber. The price of rubber had increased by 500 percent over the past few years. Rubber was suddenly a major commodity on the world market.

Because of economic and political changes, Spruce's exploration now came under the direction of the British government. He was given specific orders to obtain cuttings and seeds of the cinchona tree, the source of quinine. To do this, Spruce had to travel westward to the headwaters of the Amazon and beyond. Unlike his other journeys, this trip began in high style. Spruce had obtained passage on a river steamboat. Although he traveled in comfort, he was unhappy because the boat would not stop when he spotted a particularly attractive specimen along the shore.

The steamboat did not travel all the way to his destination and he continued by hiking through mountains and high valleys. This journey included occasional contact with a few Jivaro headhunters. The Jivaros and Spruce evidently developed a healthy mutual respect. The headhunters did not harm his party and provided them with food and drink.

Richard Spruce recognized the value of plant knowledge held by shamans and became one of the first ethnobotanists. (Courtesy of Kew Gardens, London, England)

Eventually, Spruce reached Ambato in Ecuador—a region where the cinchona tree flourishes. By this time, the collection of the bark was highly organized. Wealthy landowners controlled huge areas where cinchona trees grew wild. Spruce arranged to lease some of the land and collect the seeds as soon as they ripened. This venture required months to accomplish and needed an organized labor forced to collect the ripe seeds before they fell to the ground.

Spruce made careful notes on the climate and soil conditions in which the trees seemed to do best. When plans were made to cultivate the cinchona tree in India, where malaria is a common disease,

Spruce sent instructions to duplicate the growing conditions found in Ecuador. His advice was ignored by the British planters, and the cinchona plantations in India failed to thrive.

After fulfilling his duties to Queen Victoria, Spruce returned to Peru to continue his research. In 1864, after more bouts of malaria, he returned to England. The scientists at Kew Gardens invited Spruce to help organize the materials that he had sent back from South America. In addition, Spruce continued to work on his notes and revise the rough maps he had drawn during his expeditions.

Toward the end of his life, the British government gave Spruce a tiny pension and he retired to a cottage in Yorkshire. He died in 1893 before completing a summary of his experiences. His old friend Alfred Wallace edited his notes, and a two-volume account of his work was published in 1908. His recognition of the value of native knowledge was his key legacy. As they pursued their explorations, the scientists who entered the field after Spruce were able to save time and energy by consulting with native healers.

8

The Story of Quinine

Malaria has been known to Europeans since the beginning of recorded history. Indeed, there is some archaeological evidence from human remains that malaria was a problem during Neolithic times. Until the modern era, the disease was widespread in the Mediterranean area and greatly feared throughout Europe.

Malaria is caused by a protozoan, a microbe larger than most bacteria. The microbe is transmitted by the bite of the female *Anopheles* mosquito. Standing water must be available for the mosquito to complete its life cycle. The female lays her egg masses in bodies of water that later support the hatchlings as they mature. Therefore, any wet, swampy area can be home to the *Anopheles* mosquito.

Europeans probably first learned of quinine in 1638. At that time, the wife of the Spanish viceroy (the royal governor), Countess Chinchón, was dying of malaria in Lima, Peru. In desperation, the royal physician recommended the use of a native cure—a powdered tree bark that the natives called *quinquina*. The powder was brought 500 miles (800 km) from the village of Loja in present-day Ecuador. The native treatment was successful. When the countess returned to Spain a few years later, she took along a supply of the powdered bark. The countess retained some of the medicine for herself, but she had another use for the rest. The poorly maintained family estate—about 25 miles (40 km) south of Madrid—was low-lying and badly drained. The peasant population was constantly sickened by malarial fevers. The powdered bark cured their fevers, and the workers soon restored the land to its former productivity.

There is no clear historical evidence that the story is true. Nevertheless, European botanists named the tree that supplies the medicinal bark after the Chinchón family. The medicine was called quinine, a European form of the native word *quinquina*.

South American Indians have used quinine to cure fever-producing illnesses for untold centuries. However, malaria was unknown to South

The Anopheles *mosquito is the carrier of malaria, one of the world's major killer diseases.* (Courtesy of the Office of Communications, U.S. Department of Agriculture)

America before the Spanish conquest in 1520. Spanish soldiers who already had the disease brought it to the New World.

Jesuit missionaries, sent to convert the natives to Christianity, were the first Europeans to see quinine as a potential treatment for malaria. The missionaries lived among the native peoples in remote areas where few Europeans dared to travel. The Jesuits probably observed the natives use quinine to treat many kinds of fevers. The Jesuits sent the powder back to Spain and to Rome, the headquarters of the Catholic Church.

At first, physicians were highly suspicious of quinine and the use of the drug was confined to the clergy. A high church official, Cardinal John de Lugo, promoted the use of quinine by both his malaria-ridden parishioners and his clergy. At that time, priests rather than doctors administered quinine.

In England, opposition came not only from the medical establishment but also from the strong Protestant majority. They disliked and distrusted the Catholic Church and could not tolerate the idea that anything good could come from the Jesuits. Strangely, the man who popularized the use of quinine in England was a self-proclaimed physician—a quack by the name of Robert Talbor.

Talbor had attended Cambridge University for a brief period of time. He had some training in pharmacy and had served as an apothecary's apprentice. Talbor, a bright but unscrupulous man, recognized that the bark was quite effective. He also recognized that it could not be sold under its popular name, Jesuit Powder. Talbor simply changed the name of the powder, masked the quinine's bitter taste by adding it to wine, and set up a pharmacy in Essex—a malaria-ridden area south of London. He advertised that he had a secret formula that did not contain Jesuit Powder. Talbor also advertised that Jesuit Powder had dangerous side effects that his medicine did not produce.

Because the "secret" formula worked well, and many malaria patients were relieved of their symptoms, Talbor's reputation spread rapidly. He traveled to London at the request of wealthy malaria victims and soon grew rich. The English king Charles II became one of his supporters, in spite of the opposition of the Royal College of Physicians. The king suffered from malaria and Talbor's remedy improved his health. In gratitude, Charles gave Talbor a knighthood. The quack became Sir Robert.

Louis XIV, the king of France, became his next royal patron. Both the king and his son were victims of malaria. Their recovery was hailed throughout Europe, and Sir Robert went on to repeat his successes in Vienna and Madrid. When he returned to Paris, he was hailed as a genius. King Louis gave him an aristocratic French name, and Sir Robert Talbor became Sir Robert Talbot.

When Sir Robert expressed the wish to return to England, Louis became upset. The king did not want the secret formula to slip away. Because quinine neither prevents nor cures malaria, the king was correct in thinking his family might require further doses. (Quinine helps suppress the multiplication of the malaria microbe and thereby prevents the severe fevers associated with the body's response to the microbe.)

King Louis proposed a deal. Sir Robert wrote the formula on a piece of paper, placed the paper in an envelope, and sealed the envelope. The formula was locked away—not to be opened until after Sir Robert died. In return, the king gave Sir Robert a handsome gift of money and a life pension.

Talbor died in 1681, shortly after his return to England. When the envelope was opened, the royal personages, wealthy patrons, and physicians were embarrassed to discover that the secret ingredient had been the hated Jesuit Powder. The crafty Talbor had suspended the powdered bark of the cinchona tree in white wine where it made a bitter but acceptable elixir. People began to revise their attitude toward Jesuit Powder.

More Chemistry

In 1820, two young Frenchmen working in Paris, Joseph Pelletier and Joseph Caventou succeeded in isolating the key ingredient in quinine. They found it to be a very complicated enzyme molecule called an alkaloid. This molecule is composed of three carbon rings. Two of the rings have one atom of nitrogen and two of carbon as attachments. The third ring is unusual because the attached carbon atoms connect to a structure with an oxygen and hydrogen atom at its end.

The identification of the curative ingredient in quinine was important for three reasons. First, raw bark could be tested for its quinine content, and payment could be based on the amount of that ingredient. Second, because the active

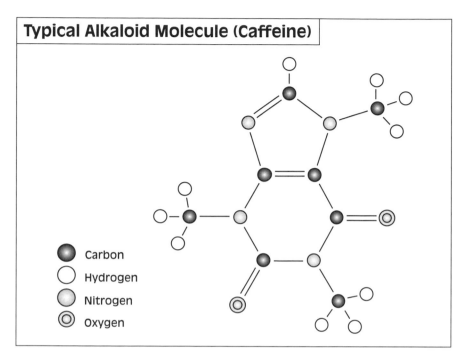

Typical Alkaloid Molecule (Caffeine)

Carbon
Hydrogen
Nitrogen
Oxygen

Many medicines are formed by small modifications of the basic alkaloid molecule.

ingredient could be weighed, doctors could prescribe the exact amount needed for proper treatment. The tendency to overdose patients was greatly reduced. The third advantage concerned the new, easier way in which quinine could be administered. The pure alkaloid could be extracted from the raw bark and formed into small pills. The bark's bitter taste was no longer a problem.

Breaking the Monopoly

The first half of the 1800s was a time of political unrest in much of Latin America. The people were fighting for their independence from European rule, and governmental authority was often lacking. Bandit groups and armed militias controlled many parts of the countryside, and this confusion interfered with the availability of quinine.

Major land owners controlled the harvesting of the wild cinchona trees and the world market depended on such supplies. The number of wild trees was rapidly decreasing because stripping away the quinine-rich bark killed the tree. Also, the transportation routes from the forests to the ports were often interrupted by local warfare. The price of cinchona bark rose as it became a scarce commodity.

The Dutch had grave problems with malaria among the colonists and native workers in the Dutch-owned East Indies, present-day Indonesia. They hoped to solve that problem and make a handsome profit by cultivating cinchona trees on Java, an island in their colony.

The Dutch government sent a botanist, J. C. Hasskarl, to collect seeds and seedlings in Peru and Bolivia. Dutch diplomats in Peru were told to make similar collections. The plant material was placed on a Dutch warship headed for present-day Jakarta, the capital of Indonesia. The voyage took a long time and few seeds or seedlings survived. Those that did produced bark with a low quinine content and the project was an economic failure.

In 1859, Clement Markham, an Englishman, persuaded his government to develop

The bark of the cinchona tree is the source of quinine, an alkaloid drug used to treat malaria. (Courtesy of Alice Tangerini and the Smithsonian Institution)

plantations of cinchona trees in India. Richard Spruce, the noted South American explorer and botanist, was assigned to collect the seeds. Although a million trees were planned for southern India and Ceylon (now Sri Lanka), the planting was poorly organized and the trees did not prosper.

Charles Ledger, a British citizen who lived in Bolivia, was the next to threaten the South American monopoly on quinine. Ledger was a professional bark dealer who employed natives to locate wild cinchona trees and harvest their bark. He assigned one of the workers to collect seeds from very productive trees. Ledger hoped to sell the seeds to the British government and thus reawaken their interest in cultivating cinchona trees. Ledger sent 14 pounds (6.3 kg) of seeds to his brother, George, who offered them for sale. The government officials had bad memories about Clement Markham's plan and declined to do business with the Ledger brothers.

George Ledger then asked the Dutch if they were interested in the seeds. Their officials were cautious but agreed to purchase a pound at a very low price. The other 13 pounds (5.9 kg) were sold to a British planter on his way to India. The planter traded them for different seeds as soon as he arrived at his destination. The 13 pounds (5.9 kg) of cinchona seeds were mishandled by the seed traders and never germinated.

The pound of seeds purchased by the Dutch was handled far more carefully. The cinchona seeds were shipped to Java, where growing conditions matched those in Peru and Bolivia. The quinine content of the healthy young plants tested three to four times higher than those from the prior plantings. The Dutch, through their greater botanical skill, had broken the South American monopoly and now controlled the most productive source of quinine.

The unfortunate native who had gathered the seeds in Bolivia was thrown into jail for violating the Bolivian prohibition against collecting cinchona seeds. Undoubtedly, the poor man was unaware that he was responsible for assuring a steady supply of one of the world's most important medicines.

Atabrine, the first synthetic medicine for malaria, was not developed until 1926. This synthetic drug helped break the Dutch dominance of the quinine market.

9

The Story of Curare

The interior of South America was avoided by early colonists because of its difficult terrain. Consequently, many of the original inhabitants were able to continue their tribal practices with few modifications. Indeed, the peoples who lived on the eastern slopes of the Andes Mountains and in the rain forests were almost totally free from European interference. Their villages were populated by extended family groups and sustained by some farming, hunting, fishing, and the gathering of wild fruits and vegetables. Hunters used both bows with arrows and blowguns with small darts. Often, the tips of the darts and arrows were coated with a dark brown poisonous paste. This poison has many names but is known in the English-speaking world as curare.

Initial Explorations

Spaniards and other Europeans were intrigued by curare from the beginning of colonization. The Spanish explorer Francisco de Orellana wrote about the effects of curare in 1541. He noted that when the poison enters the bloodstream of a bird or animal it generates a general paralysis that is followed by death.

The Spanish were unsuccessful in their attempts to learn more about this strange substance. Because the native peoples had often been treated badly by the Spanish, it is not surprising that they refused to share their recipes for making curare. Over the years, a few explorers managed to obtain samples of the dark brown paste, but no one could obtain the recipe and no one could isolate the ingredients. Though the effects of curare were little understood, scientists speculated that this potent poison might have a possible use in medicine. They knew that curare induces a total relaxation of all muscles except the heart. Therefore, some reasoned that the substance might be used to treat diseases such as epilepsy that cause dangerous muscle spasms.

Setting the Stage

An Englishman named Charles Waterton was one of the first to actively pursue the idea that curare could be used in a medicine. Waterton had inherited large farming estates in Yorkshire, England, and was responsible for the family's sugar plantations in present-day Guyana, a small country on the northeastern coast of South America. His plantations were on the Demerara River near Georgetown, the capital of the country.

In 1810, while Waterton was managing the family's Guyanan plantations, he had an encounter with the local police. They were seeking a friend of Waterton's in connection with some bad debts. Waterton refused to help the police in their quest and was soon called before the governor-general of the colony. When Waterton did not deny his actions, the governor-general was impressed by his courage and released him. The official later became Waterton's friend and awarded him a permit to explore the upper reaches of the Demerara River.

Waterton, a widower in his late 20s, was an adventurous person. He was a notable hunter and amateur naturalist. He was also a field biologist with a great interest in birds. Waterton saw his trip up the Demerara River and into the interior as a major opportunity to search for new species of birds.

As a hunter, Waterton was aware of the use of curare by the native peoples and was curious about its properties. He thought that curare might provide a cure for tetanus, rabies, and other diseases that induce powerful muscle spasms. Waterton also had ideas about how accidental curare poisoning might be remedied.

Perhaps because the natives he encountered had had no previous contact with Europeans, the young adventurer learned more about curare poison than any previous explorer. Waterton was given samples of the material and shown how it was prepared. He learned that the main ingredient was obtained by stewing pieces of a certain woody vine in boiling water. Other plant materials were then added to make it gluey, and ingredients such as ants and pepper pods were added for dramatic effect.

Waterton took some of the curare back to England. After he returned to his home in Yorkshire, he tested one of his ideas about the effects of the poison. Waterton demonstrated that his donkey could be kept alive by artificial respiration after being injected with the poison. His crude—but successful—artificial respiration technique involved pumping air into the animal's lungs by using a bellows borrowed from the family fireplace. He proved that the effect of the poison was short-lived and that a victim could survive if administered oxygen during the time of paralysis. However, the short duration of the poison's effect meant that chronic diseases with persistent muscle spasms were not helped by curare. Repeated doses—to extend the period of relief—were too dangerous for the patient. Waterton's donkey was unwell for about one year after her experience with curare.

Solving the Curare Puzzle

Although curare was not useful as a cure for chronic muscle seizures, some members of the medical profession continued to show an interest in the substance. Over the following century, doctors and chemists in Europe and South America requested samples for testing their ideas. Chemists kept trying, unsuccessfully, to isolate the active ingredients. Some physicians used small amounts of the material to moderate the cramped muscles caused by severe arthritis. However, most doctors were afraid to prescribe the poorly understood compound.

In the 1930s, interest in curare began to surface again. About that same time, Richard Gill, a young American from Washington, D.C., became curious about the substance. Gill and his wife, Ruth, owned and operated a ranch in Ecuador. The ranch was located in the valley of the Río Pastaza, about a day's horseback ride from the nearest town. Although somewhat isolated, the ranch was on a major thoroughfare for natives traveling between the eastern slope of the Andes and the tropical jungles that grew in the plain. Gill came to know all the frequent travelers. He also became friends with the local Quichua Indians who worked for him, and he learned their language.

Gill's interest in native medicines was aroused when Ruth had a bad fall. Gill was preparing to carry her by stretcher into the nearest town when one of the ranch hands declared that the long, difficult trek might not be necessary. The elderly Indian said he had studied with local shamans and had traveled, in his youth, to the territory of the feared Jívaro tribe, noted for its drug-making skills. Gill was persuaded to let the Indian treat his wife in the local manner. When Ruth recovered after the treatment, Gill was convinced that there were healing powers in native medicines.

Years later, when Gill was back in the United States on a vacation, he experienced symptoms of multiple sclerosis (MS), a degenerative disease of the central nervous system. An attending physician mentioned that curare might provide at least some release from the crippling pain and tremors of MS. The doctor also remarked that the identity of the active ingredient in curare was unknown and dosage control was difficult.

When asked, the doctor told Gill that the supply of the raw plant materials was insufficient for an extensive chemical analysis of curare.

Gill resolved to overcome his physical disability, return to Ecuador, and learn the secrets of curare from the Indians. He was confident that he could discover which plants were used to make the substance and the methods to manufacture it.

While Gill convalesced, he wrote popular articles about his interest in curare and his adventures as an Ecuadorian rancher. In 1938, Sayre Merrill, a wealthy New England businessman, read one of his stories. Merrill offered to sponsor an expedition with Gill as leader. After careful planning and preparation, Gill and his wife returned to Ecuador.

Gill had been gone for six years and his property was not in good condition. He rehired his farmhands and quickly restored the ranch. Using his home as a base, Gill recruited nearly 100 local men. He also purchased or hired mules and horses to carry supplies and trading goods into the interior. After everything was organized, they headed east into a jungle region called the Pacayacu. Because of his disability, Gill had some difficulty negotiating jungle trails in the Andean foothills and the progress was a slow. After a few days, they reached one of the tributaries of the Amazon River, where they traveled faster and more comfortably by dugout canoes. In order to preserve the secrecy of his sources, Gill never revealed which tributary he embarked upon.

Gill sought a major village of the Jívaro people. These natives were noted for their use of curare and their resistance to outside influences. In spite of their reputation for hostility, Gill gained the confidence of the village leaders. Ultimately, he was allowed to observe the full ritual of curare preparation. Gill learned that the villagers used as many as six different plants in the preparation. Three plants were used in the first stage of brewing and the bark of a fourth was added after the mixture had boiled for a while. Two days later, two more plants were added and the stew was slowly boiled down to a dark brown paste.

After comparing several different recipes, Gill discovered that the one common ingredient was vinelike plant with a stem that measured three to five inches (8 to 13 cm) in diameter. As Waterton had reported about 100 years before, the vine was cut into short lengths and stewed to extract the critical ingredient.

When Gill and his wife left the jungle after their three-month adventure, they carried samples of the plant and the semiprocessed poison. They returned to New York City, where Gill wanted to start a business trading in curare and the raw materials from which curare is extracted. Gill expected to retain his monopoly on the curare market because no one else had gained the cooperation of the Jívaro people.

At first, as in Waterton's time, the medical community was enthusiastic about the possible uses of curare. Some specialists hoped that it might help in the treatment of epilepsy and other diseases. The major pharmaceutical houses, however, soon lost interest. Scientists rediscovered the fact that the drug's actions were too transient. After receiving a dose of the medicine, a patient's muscle spasms decreased but the drug's effect soon wore off. Curare was classified as a palliative—a medicine that reduces the pain of a medical condition.

A few years later, however, the drug was proven to be invaluable in the medication of surgery patients. Surgeons needed a way to relax muscles—particularly of the abdomen—during operations. Ordinary anesthesia might put the patient to sleep and deaden the pain sensations but did little to relax tensed muscles. Curare worked well for this purpose. Its short-lived effects were ideal because physicians wanted muscle tone to return as soon as the operation was completed.

In spite of this important development, Gill never became a major trader in curare or its raw materials. The large pharmaceutical houses developed their own suppliers and immediately broke Gill's monopoly. He tried unsuccessfully to find a backer to finance another, grander expedition into the Amazon region.

The National Research Council proposed a government-funded project. Dr. Robert Griggs was chosen to be leader and Gill was offered the position of field assistant. Because Gill was not a trained scientist, Griggs thought that Gill could contribute little to a scientific expedition. Therefore, Gill was assigned to guide the group and make contact with the local tribes. He was insulted and disappointed and presented his grievance to a government panel. No verdict was reached because the National Research Council withdrew their proposal for the expedition.

Gill moved to California and supported himself by importing and reselling curare paste and other tropical products. In his garage laboratory, he worked on new ways to employ curare. Richard Gill died in 1958 of complications of the disease that he had acquired 20 years before. Through his efforts, curare became an important medical asset. Curare's greatest contribution to health care is the use of its active ingredients as chemical building blocks. One of the active agents was found to be a perfect catalyst in the synthesis of a fast-acting anesthetic.

In modern times, the mystery of the raw materials and chemical composition of curare has been solved. Field botanists and anthropologists learned that at least seven different plants can be used as the principal raw material for making curare. Different native groups use different combinations of raw materials as well as different incidental ingredients. Consequently, there may be hundreds of recipes for curare and probably no two batches are exactly the same—even if prepared by the same shaman.

The identification of the key active ingredient was difficult and time consuming. At first, chemists were mystified when each new sample of raw curare yielded a totally different group of components. They expected to find one common active ingredient. Although the seven main plant materials all cause rapid general muscle relaxation, the active ingredients of each material have slightly different chemical compositions. The chemists finally realized that they were dealing with not one but several highly similar alkaloid molecules that produced the same physical effects.

10
Hormones

Some molecules manufactured by the human body are closely paralleled by some molecules produced by plants. In many cases, a plant-derived molecule can block the actions of a chemical produced by the human body. When morphine, heroin, or other drugs derived from the opium poppy are introduced into an individual, their molecules block chemicals that help keep the person alert and sensitive to pain. Consequently, the person becomes drowsy and anesthetized.

In addition to blocking the effects of some of the body's natural chemicals, plant molecules can substitute for the catalysts in the human body. Catalysts are essential to life because they activate vital chemical reactions. Enzymes are catalysts that cause molecules to form necessary compounds. Hormones—from a Greek word that means "urge on"—are also catalysts but serve a different function. A hormone is produced by one human organ and then carried by the bloodstream to a different organ. As the Greek word implies, the hormone then "urges on," or stimulates—by acting as a catalyst—that second organ to produce certain chemicals. Serious diseases such as diabetes result when the body fails to manufacture enough of a particular hormone. Over the past 150 years, scientists have identified all or nearly all of the vital hormones. Fortunately, hormone substitutes made from plants or synthetic materials can act as exact copies of many of the missing hormones and allow a human body to function properly.

Human organs known as endocrine glands produce dozens of hormones that support various body functions such as storing energy and activating muscles. In some ways, these hormones are similar to vitamins in that only a small quantity is needed at any one time—but that small quantity is very important. The hormones control various nonglandular organs and allow one hormone to regulate the amount of another hormone in the system. Scientists have thoroughly investigated the hormonal activity of the adrenal gland and the reproductive organs and have searched for plant-derived or synthetic hormones to mimic the natural effects. Over the years, they have arrived at some far-reaching conclusions.

The Adrenal Glands

The interior of the adrenal glands produces two hormones of major significance—epinephrine and nor-epinephrine. (These hormones are also known as adrenaline and nor-adrenaline.) They are released when the body senses a severe physical threat. The brain recognizes the threat and the nervous system triggers these hormones. Indeed, there is a strong link between these glands and the nervous system. Epinephrine and nor-epinephrine activate the "fight or flight" reflexes. In other words, when the two hormones are released, the human body is ready to fight a "battle" or run the other way. The nervous system acts to draw fuel from the liver, increase the heart rate and blood pressure, and—in general—pep up the body for intense activity.

The significance of the adrenal glands was discovered by Dr. Thomas Addison, who was born in Scotland and studied medicine there. In 1855, when Addison was on the surgical staff of Guy's Hospital in London, England, he noted a mysterious, often fatal illness. The patients suffered from a general weakness, anemia, and a yellowing of the skin. Many cases were so alike that Dr. Addison correctly concluded that he was seeing

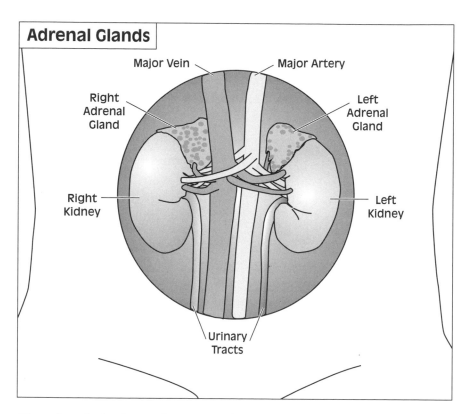

Adrenal Glands

Major Vein

Major Artery

Right Adrenal Gland

Left Adrenal Gland

Right Kidney

Left Kidney

Urinary Tracts

The adrenal glands are the source of many hormones; they sit atop the kidneys.

the effects of one particular disease. After the patients died, he conducted detailed autopsies of the bodies and found only one factor in common: each autopsy showed that the small oval organs that lay over each kidney were severely shriveled. Addison concluded that the disease was caused by the malfunction of these organs—the adrenal glands. The condition has been named Addison's disease after the man who identified the cause.

Later, an American of French ancestry named Charles Brown-Sequard showed that animals do not survive after the removal of their adrenal glands. In short, these seemingly insignificant organs are essential to life. Unfortunately, neither Addison nor Brown-Sequard were able to determine why these organs were so important.

An Adrenaline Mimic

Thousands of years ago, people in China brewed a tea made from a wiry-stemmed plant called *ma huang* in the Chinese language. The modern botanical name for the plant is *Ephedra sinica*. The tea was a famous stimulant and used in ancient times for the treatment of hay fever and related breathing problems. Teas made from closely related plants were drunk over the course of time by many peoples in many places. Indeed, tea made from a close relative of *Ephedra sinica* was brewed by the Greeks and Romans. In A.D. 60, the Roman naturalist Pliny the Elder wrote a description of the tea's effects.

A similar plant was discovered by the pioneers who built the American southwest. They used another member of the *Ephedra* genus for their stimulating tea. Thus, for centuries,

Stems and leaves of the female ephedra plant shown here have been used to make a stimulating tea by many people in different parts of the world. However, it has proven harmful when used as a means of weight control. The U.S. Food and Drug Administration now restricts its distribution and use. (Courtesy of James Manhart, Texas A&M University)

some form of ephedra tea was a common folk remedy although no one understood how or why it worked. As usual, there are many stories—both true and false—about popular folk remedies. Ephedra tea was once thought to be a cure for syphilis. In reality, the plant had no curative effect on that disease.

In 1885, the active ingredient in ma huang was isolated by Japanese scientists. The ingredient, an alkaloid, was purified in 1887 and named ephedrine. Around 1924, an American and a Chinese-American physiologist conducted clinical tests on the compound while working at Peking Union Medical College. The two men had held a long-standing interest in Chinese folk medicine. Their introduction of ephedrine into standard medical procedure was a major success. For example, it is used to treat the symptoms of asthma and as a heart stimulant in cases of acute heart stoppage.

Chemists soon discovered that ephedrine—the plant product—has a chemical makeup and properties similar to epinephrine—the human product. The two chemicals are both alkaloids and share the same basic molecular structure. The plant-derived medication, however, has some advantages. Ephedrine can be taken by mouth while epinephrine loses its effectiveness in the digestive system and must be administered by injection. For some conditions, such as asthma, ephedrine is the better choice. Both the animal hormone and the plant hormone can be used in the treatment of several conditions including sudden heart failure. If the heart stops beating because of a severe injury or an overdose of drugs, paramedics usually administer epinephrine or ephedrine along with electrical stimulation to restart a heart beat.

Once the chemical connection between epinephrine and ephedrine was made clear, chemists began to study similar alkaloids. They added and subtracted combinations of atoms that were connected to the basic alkaloid structure of epinephrine. This work soon led to the development of benzedrine and a growing family of amphetamines—called pep pills—all derived from the plant material, ephedrine. The "rush" some people experience when riding a roller coaster is imitated by benzedrine and the other amphetamines. This effect leads to some misuse of these drugs.

The Adrenal Cortex

When the adrenal glands were found to be the source of powerful hormones such as epinephrine (adrenaline), scientists began to search for other hormones. In 1924, researchers at Johns Hopkins Hospital in Baltimore, Maryland, proved that Addison's disease is not caused by a shortage of epinephrine— as Addison had believed. Instead, the illness is caused by a lack of material from the cortex (outer skin) of the adrenal gland. Studies found that the cortex of the adrenal glands produces dozens of complicated chemical compounds. The compounds counteract inflammations, allergies, and the negative effects of stress and are more important to the human body than adrenaline. In 1935, a pure extract of the outer skin of the adrenal glands was produced by scientists at the Upjohn Company. By 1940, 40 of the 46 distinct compounds in this extract had been isolated and identified.

The Search for Cortisone

Today, cortisone is produced in large quantities and at low cost from plants such as the Mexican yam. However, it was very rare until the 1960s. In late 1941, just after the United States had entered World War II, a strange rumor circulated among the military services. The rumor indicated that German bomber pilots were being given an extract from the adrenal cortex to counter the effects of high-altitude flights. This rumor was false but it mobilized the U.S. research establishment. Scientists soon realized that every cow and pig in the country would lose their adrenal glands if the government ordered enough extract to treat all U.S. bomber pilots. That project was not too practical and a synthetic substitute was sought.

The first attempts to find a substitute for the extract from the adrenal cortex used a compound found in the bile of cattle—a waste product of the beef industry. This compound is closely related to cholesterol. Researchers at Merck and Company, the drug manufacturer, used as many as 60 steps to complete the synthesis. The scientists synthesized a few grams of three different chemicals produced naturally by the adrenal cortex. By the time this work was completed, World War II was over. Most of the chemicals were used to treat victims of Addison's disease, but a few grams were put into storage in the laboratory.

In 1948, Dr. Philip S. Hench at the Mayo Clinic in Rochester, Minnesota, observed that some female patients with severe arthritis showed great improvement if they became pregnant. Some patients with jaundice showed the same effect. At first, the connection between pregnancy and the relief of symptoms of arthritis or jaundice was not clear. In searching for a link, researchers surmised that the improvement might be due to a stress reaction. Pregnancy or jaundice might be a source of stress that activated the adrenal glands. The glands, in turn, might produce a hormone that reduced the swelling and inflammation of arthritis or improved the condition of a jaundiced, pregnant woman.

When a patient with severe symptoms of arthritis was admitted to the clinic, Hench decided to test his ideas. He obtained a small sample of the chemicals that had been produced by the Merck scientists. Using a fraction of the compound, he made a solution and injected it into the vein of the patient. After two days of treatment, the patient's pain, stiffness, and swollen joints were gone. The material, which had been labeled Kendall's Compound E, was soon renamed cortisone.

Medical applications of cortisone grew rapidly, but the supply remained tiny. The only commercial source was an extract made from the bile removed from slaughtered cattle. No major drug firm had been able to invent a new way to mass-produce cortisone.

The Testes

In the meantime, other human glands were being investigated and scientists were reading earlier studies on the subject. In 1849, the German physiologist Arnold Berthold demonstrated that masculine behavior could be restored to a castrated chicken when testes from another male chicken were surgically implanted. This research showed that male sex organs did more than produce sperm. The "foreign" testes contributed some substance to the rooster's body that activated male patterns of behavior. However, at that time, no one could identify the substance. In 1927, almost 75 years later, a chemical was extracted from bulls' testes and administered to castrated roosters. The chemical restored the roosters' masculine behavior. Because the material was effective in a different species of animal, the scientists, F. C. Koch and L. C. McGee, proved that the chemical extracted from the testes was a universal restorative of masculine characteristics.

The work of Koch and McGee was published in 1927 but another eight years were needed to identify the chemical structure of the substance. The masculinity-inducing hormone was actually two slightly different chemicals—androsterone and testosterone. They belong to the chemical family of steroids, fatlike materials that include cholesterol. Biochemists have recently shown that both male and female hormones use cholesterol as a raw material.

When a man's body cannot produce a sufficient amount of testosterone, an injection of the male hormone can restore masculine characteristics and functions. The same hormone has the ability to activate muscle growth. After stomach surgery, patients often lose their appetites and suffer from malnutrition. They cannot manufacture sufficient protein to build muscle tissue. Indeed, their muscles slowly deteriorate as muscle cells die and are not replaced.

Injections of male hormones restore the patient's appetite and the ability to manufacture and use proteins. Weight loss is stopped and muscles begin to grow. The use of male hormones is of special interest to doctors who treat young children for nervous disorders and failure to develop good musculature. Unfortunately, the hormone treatments that build bodies also bring about secondary sex characteristics such as facial hair. Chemists began to seek synthetics that would have the positive effects of the natural hormone but would not masculinize young children and female patients. Such synthetics were achieved by scientists at the Searle Company in 1955.

These synthetic male hormones are particularly effective in treating burn victims. When young children are badly burned, the hormones are especially helpful in healing large blisters and speeding recovery.

The Ovaries

Almost 50 years after the experiment with a transplanted rooster testes revealed the function of the male hormone, a similar experiment was conducted by transplanting ovaries. The studies were done in Austria in 1896. However, the effects of ovarian extracts were not demonstrated until 1923. Several more years were needed to isolate the active ingredient. This was finally achieved during the search for a quick and easy pregnancy test. Two German scientists found that if the urine of a pregnant woman was injected into an immature rabbit, the rabbit would become sexually receptive. The new test seemed to show that a pregnant woman's urine contained a fair amount of the female hormone. So, chemists began to analyze samples of the urine to isolate the hormone. They soon discovered that the urine of pregnant female horses also contained the female hormone and was more easily obtainable. Therefore, horse urine became the raw material of choice. Pure crystals of the female hormone, estrone, were isolated in 1929. Shortly after, two other female hormones were identified and isolated—estrogen and progesterone.

The main application for these female hormones was to regularize the menstrual cycle, which can be upset by illness, injury, or other sources of stress. However, in the 1940s and early 1950s, the most important use for estrogen was to help childless women become pregnant. Through the administration of rather large doses of the hormone, patients were induced to experience a "false" pregnancy. For several months, symptoms such as morning sickness were artificially induced. Scientists hoped that the body of the potential mother would initiate pregnancy-like conditions in the womb and other organs. In other words, the body would have a rehearsal for being pregnant. When the hormone injections were stopped, the body was better prepared for a real pregnancy. This scheme worked for a large proportion of infertile patients.

Doctors found that during a false pregnancy—induced by the hormone injections—and a real pregnancy women stopped producing eggs. This discovery instigated the development of the contraceptive pill—a medication that prevents women from becoming pregnant.

Up until the late 1940s and early 1950s, all the sex hormones and cortisone, the close chemical relative of the sex hormone, were in short supply. These materials were all derived from animal sources. However, the supply problem was solved by the efforts of several chemists who discovered that these hormones could be produced from plant extracts in large amounts at low cost. This change of raw material source has had and continues to have major societal effects in the areas of disease prevention and cure and in the control of human reproduction.

11
Synthesis

In 1940, an important historical document was brought to light by Dr. E. W. Emmart, a professor of medicine from Johns Hopkins University in Baltimore, Maryland. While visiting the Vatican Library in Rome, Dr. Emmart, an ardent Catholic and book lover, came across a little-known work called the Badianus Manuscript. In the early 1550s, the author, an Aztec physician, had compiled a complete list of all the medicinal plants used in traditional Aztec medicines. The document, which he wrote while teaching in central Mexico, contained descriptions of more than 250 plants. The manuscripts included information about whether a particular plant was cultivated or grew wild. It also told how the medicinal ingredients were extracted and how the medicines were used in the treatment of various diseases.

In 1552, the book was translated from the Aztec language into Latin by a native named Juan Badiano and the translation was then sent to Spain. The history of its journey to the Vatican Library is unknown. Dr. Emmart's discovery of that 400-year-old manuscript generated new public and professional interest in natural products and folk medicine.

Russell Marker

One of the plants mentioned in the Aztec herbal was the Central American yam. This plant is not to be confused with the sweet potato that is sometimes called a yam in North America. Some Central American yams are edible but most of the 400 species are either unpalatable or poisonous. In fact, a fish poison is made from the mashed root of certain species. When the substance is released into a lake or river, the fish in the immediate area are killed quickly, but their flesh remains wholesome. Other species of yams produce a juice that foams like soap and the natives use it for washing clothing.

In 1940, the same year that the Badianus Manuscript stimulated an interest in medicinal plants, a biochemist named Russell E. Marker was working on a new line of research. For some time, he had been thinking about synthesizing hormones—particularly female sex hormones such as estrogen and progesterone.

Scientists knew that the symptoms of rheumatoid arthritis in a female patient were significantly relieved if she became pregnant. There was a strong theory that the pregnancy-related increase in progesterone—a female hormone—was the key factor in reducing the symptoms. The sex hormones and cortisone are members of the family of chemicals known as steroids. The steroid molecules are similar to cholesterol and are composed of four rings made up of carbon, oxygen, and hydrogen atoms.

In the early 1940s, male and female hormones and cortisone were difficult to obtain and extremely expensive. At the same time, scientists knew that hundreds of natural steroids were readily available from a variety of plants including the Mexican yam. Marker thought that perhaps a species of yam might supply the perfect steroid to facilitate the synthesis of hormones—particularly progesterone.

Marker had been studying natural steroids for years. He was on the chemistry faculty at Pennsylvania State University and worked part-time for a major pharmaceutical house. Over the years, he had written more than 150 research reports and had received more than 75 patents on steroid chemistry.

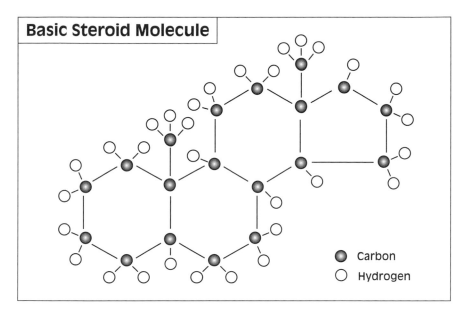

Basic Steroid Molecule

● Carbon
○ Hydrogen

The steroid molecule is the building block for cholesterol and several hormones such as cortisone and the gender hormones.

In addition to his other talents, Marker had learned to be a competent field botanist by spending his vacations in Mexico, making surveys of growing plants, and gathering information about the properties of local plants—particularly the yams.

Marker was most interested in the steroid diosgenin, closely related to sapogenin, used by villagers as soap. He discovered that the best source of diosgenin was a yam that grew from a rough-skinned, dark brown rhizome or potato-like root. The root usually weighs about four pounds (2 kg), but older plants have larger roots that can weigh more than 100 pounds (45 kg). Marker had found the ideal raw material for his experiments.

In 1943, Marker resigned from his professional positions and moved to Mexico. Just outside Mexico City, he rented a modest shed to use as his chemistry laboratory. Using a secret process, he produced more than four pounds (2 kg) of pure progesterone in a few months. At the time, progesterone's wholesale price was about $40,000 a pound. Marker sold all four pounds (2 kg) to Laboratorios Hormona, a Mexican company established 10 years before by two European refugees. The owners purchased Marker's homemade progesterone and offered him a partnership in Syntex, their newly formed company. Syntex broke the European virtual monopoly on progesterone and reduced its price by 90 percent.

At first, all went well with the partnership. Soon, however, it became apparent that Marker was a difficult person and did not relate well with the others. The partners bought out Marker's share of the business in 1945. Once again, Marker worked on his own and after some initial success dropped out of public view.

The tuberous roots of the Mexican yam, sometimes weighing as much as 50 pounds (about 21 kg), are the source of a steroid that can be converted into several different hormones. (Courtesy of James Manhart, Texas A&M University)

Meanwhile, the founders of Syntex hired another European refugee, George Rosenkrantz, a Swiss-educated Hungarian. In 1951, Rosenkrantz hired Karl Djerassi, a young expatriate Bulgarian, already well regarded as a steroid chemist. Djerassi and Rosenkrantz immediately began research on a process to synthesize cortisone from yams.

Karl Djerassi

Djerassi was born in 1923 and lived in Sofia, Bulgaria, until his parents divorced. After the divorce, when Karl was six years old, his mother, an oral surgeon, returned to her home city of Vienna, Austria. Until the beginnings of World War II, Karl spent the school year in Vienna with his mother and summers in Bulgaria with his father. His father, also a physician, was a specialist in chronic diseases.

In 1939, when Hitler took over Austria, Karl's parents remarried so that the boy and his mother could claim Bulgarian citizenship. Their new passports allowed them to escape first to Sofia and then to the United States. After arriving in New York, they were helped by the Hebrew Sheltering and Immigrant Aid Society. Karl's mother found a job as a medical assistant in rural New York State.

Karl, who had had only two years of secondary education in Europe, decided to begin his higher education as soon as possible. He wanted to become a physician. In December, Karl went to see a friend of his father's who was a faculty member at New York University (NYU). Karl was advised to apply to Newark Junior College in New Jersey since NYU did not accept students in the middle of a school year. His transcript from the American College of Sofia—a school that he attended briefly—persuaded the officials at the New Jersey college that Karl had had at least one year of higher education. He was accepted at the junior college.

He realized quickly that the Newark Junior College was not a good springboard for a career in medicine. However, he took the premedical science curriculum and was inspired by the chemistry teacher to consider chemistry as a career choice. In the meantime, he applied for a foreign student scholarship from the Institute of International Education. He obtained the scholarship and was accepted at a small four-year institution, Tarkio College in Tarkio, Missouri.

Through a series of strange coincidences, Karl became a frequent speaker at church suppers. He always spoke on the "current situation in Europe." Perhaps because of his foreign accent, he was well received. Actually, he knew little about the subject and got most of his ideas from John Gunther's book, *Inside Europe.* The donations given by audiences at the churches or luncheon clubs kept him in pocket money while he was at Tarkio.

Djerassi learned that he was being considered for a scholarship at Kenyon College in Gambier, Ohio. That June, he stopped to visit the school on the way to his mother's home in upstate New York. He fell in love with the Episcopalian institution and was delighted to accept the scholarship. Kenyon had an outstanding chemistry faculty, and Djerassi soon decided to change his major from premed to chemistry.

Djerassi was 18 when he finished his degree. He had attended Kenyon for two semesters (with extra-heavy course loads) and a summer term. Djerassi was not called into the military service because of an old knee injury. Therefore, he was free to find a job or continue his education.

After graduation, he went to visit his mother in Ellenburg Center, New York. While there, he read some publicity material from pharmaceutical companies and realized that many of them had production facilities in nearby New Jersey. He sent letters of application to the research departments of several of the companies. Most did not answer his letters, but he was invited for an interview by the CIBA Corporation.

Djerassi was hired and assigned to be an assistant to Charles Hutterer—a fellow refugee from Vienna. Hutterer soon succeeded in synthesizing pyribenzamine, one of the first effective antihistamines—a medication that relieves the symptoms of colds and allergies. Djerassi was included in the list of inventors on the patent application and as an author on the scientific report published by the American Chemical Society. He also worked on projects in the area of steroid chemistry and took graduate courses at night school at both NYU and Brooklyn Polytechnical Institute. He realized that part-time graduate work was a poor way to get a doctoral degree. Djerassi applied to the Wisconsin Alumni Research Foundation for a fellowship. He was awarded the fellowship, and CIBA Corporation gave him a small grant.

At the University of Wisconsin, he was influenced by two steroid chemists, William S. Johnson and Alfred L. Wilds. The latter became Djerassi's dissertation adviser and the former a valued friend. His dissertation concerned the transformation of testosterone, the male hormone, into a female hormone, estrogen.

Djerassi received his Ph.D. from Wisconsin in two years and returned to his job at CIBA. CIBA was a generous employer and allowed its scientists to work on their own project for one day each week. Djerassi was able to publish reports on his own research. He hoped to gain a faculty appointment and publications are necessary to fulfill that ambition. In spite of his good work, he was not offered a position by any top-notch academic institution.

So, Djerassi remained at CIBA. By 1949, the therapeutic properties of cortisone were being investigated. Djerassi wanted to work on cortisone synthesis because of his interest in steroid chemistry. However, CIBA's managers decided to conduct their cortisone research at their headquarters in Switzerland. He was disappointed in this development and began to look around for a position that would give him more freedom. He heard of an opening as a codirector of research at Syntex, a small pharmaceutical company in Mexico City.

A little-known firm such as Syntex seemed a foolish move for someone as ambitious as Djerassi. However, they paid for his visit to Mexico City, and he could not refuse the offer of an interesting journey. When he arrived at Mexico City, he was met by another expatriate Eastern European, the Hungarian George Rosenkrantz. The two shared more than an Eastern European background. They were both young and highly ambitious.

The Syntex laboratory was well equipped—far better than Djerassi had expected. Perhaps the combination of Rosenkrantz, Djerassi, and the Syntex Company would gain the shining reputation that they all craved. Djerassi accepted the appointment in spite of the skepticism of his former colleagues at the University of Wisconsin.

At that time, Djerassi's friends did not know that Rosenkrantz had furthered the pioneering work of Russell Marker. Not only did Syntex use the yam to supply progesterone to large drug companies, but Rosenkrantz had employed Marker's ideas to produce the male hormone testosterone from the same Mexican yams. Because testosterone was an expensive material, the little company was quite prosperous before Djerassi arrived on the scene. This good cash flow allowed Rosenkrantz and Djerassi to operate a double shift in the laboratory. Each senior researcher had a team of four chemists to conduct the time-consuming work involved in shifting the molecular structure of the diosogenin to that of the hormone. By June 1951, they succeeded in producing pure cortisone from the diosogenin. This achievement made Syntex a world leader in steroid chemistry—but Djerassi was not finished.

In a few months' time, Djerassi and his team of chemists had synthesized a hormone called norethindrone that stops the production of eggs in human females. This hormone became the foundation for the production of an oral contraceptive. By the early 1960s, Syntex was the major supplier for that rapidly growing market.

By this time, Syntex had become a research partner with a major U.S. drug firm and soon was purchased by financiers based in New York City. The Mexican government attempted to extract as much money as possible from the successful Syntex Company. They imposed high tariffs on the export of the steroids and the raw yams. Then, the government took over yam production in Mexico. With this act, the government had gone too far. U.S. drug companies that produced or marketed steroids found alternative sources for their ingredients. The investors encouraged Djerassi to move to California, take a faculty position at Stanford University in Palo Alto, and continue his research away from Mexican officials.

Percy L. Julian

In the meantime, other outstanding biochemists were using a different approach to the problem of cortisone production. One such noted scientist was Percy Julian.

Percy Julian was born in the spring of 1899 in Montgomery, Alabama, as the oldest of six children. His father was a railway mail clerk and his grandfather and great-grandfather had been slaves. Both the old men were alive when Percy was growing up and their wit and knowledge inspired him in many ways.

At that time, there were no high schools for African-American children in Montgomery. The nearest secondary school had been established to train teachers for the segregated elementary schools. Percy and his family hoped that this school would provide a good preparation for college. They were disappointed in the curriculum because it offered little instruction in the sciences. Indeed, when Percy was offered a partial scholarship at DePauw University in

The poisonous beans of the Calabar vine are the source of eye medicine and were formerly used in tribal ceremonies to determine the guilt or innocence of a person accused of a crime. (Courtesy of the New York Botanical Garden)

Greencastle, Indiana, he was not properly prepared for college-level work. He was admitted on probation and remained in that situation for almost three years.

During his entire college career, he supplemented his small stipend by waiting tables at a fraternity house. Some of the time, he worked as a laborer during the day and attended classes in the evenings. Despite these difficulties, Percy loved the school. He encouraged his two brothers and his three sisters to enroll at DePauw. Ultimately, the entire family—mother, father, sisters and brothers—all moved to Greencastle.

After he graduated in 1920, Julian was employed by Fisk University as an instructor in chemistry. While at Fisk, he encouraged many young African Americans to seek careers in science.

In 1922, Percy Julian was awarded a fellowship to Harvard University and received his master's degree in 1923. For a time, he worked at Harvard as a research assistant to one of the top organic chemists. Following that job, he taught at an all-black school, West Virginia State College.

Another fellowship was soon available to Julian. This was a prestigious Rockefeller grant to study for a doctoral degree in chemistry at the Chemische Institut in Vienna, Austria. After receiving his doctorate, Julian collaborated for several years with an Austrian colleague, Josef Pikl.

Julian spent two years at Howard University in Washington, D.C., after returning from Europe. His next position was at DePauw, his undergraduate college. Julian taught in the chemistry department and conducted research. This was a turning point for him. Research became so vitally important to Julian that he and his friend Pikl spent all their time working on the delicate synthesis of physostigmine. This alkaloid, derived from the Calabar bean, is used in the treatment of glaucoma, an eye disease that can cause blindness.

Julian and Pikl were soon in competition with a team of British scientists. The British team was working on an alternative approach to the synthesis of physostigmine. Julian disputed some of their results. In fact, he stated publicly that the British researchers were wrong. His career was at risk unless he could prove his accusations. To do that, he had to show that he had assembled the correct molecule of physostigmine and the British had produced something else. In February 1935, the two synthetic materials were matched with the natural material. Julian's product was shown to be identical.

Percy Julian found a way to extract cortisone from soybean oil. (Courtesy of the American Chemical Society)

The oil of the Calabar bean is also a source of stigmasterol—another natural steroid from which sex hormones can be constructed. Julian succeeded in isolating the steroid from the oil by using a mild acid wash. He wanted to evaluate the effectiveness of the wash by using soybean oil, a more plentiful and less expensive raw material. Julian ordered five pounds (2 kg) of soybean oil from the Glidden Company to carry on his research. Shortly, he received his shipment of the oil and a job offer from Glidden. The company bosses had been following Julian's career and had been impressed with his ability—especially his handling of the British competition. He decided to postpone his acid wash tests and accepted Glidden's proposal. The new job led to other research on soybean oil, which later produced both sex hormones and cortisone.

12
Ethnobotany Comes of Age

In the mid-1800s, Richard Spruce had demonstrated that the peoples of the Amazon area were highly astute in their identification of medicinal plants. He spent most of his adult life in South America and faced many problems—such as bouts with malaria—to bring back hundreds of plants for study by European scientists. For many years, no one followed in his footsteps. Finally, a young botanist from Harvard took up the challenge.

Richard Evans Schultes

Dick Schultes was born on January 12, 1915, in Boston, Massachusetts. He grew up in East Boston, a working-class neighborhood across the Chelsea Creek from the center of the city. His mother's father was a master mechanic at a local shipyard. His father's father was a former German military officer who worked as a drayman for a brewery, delivering barrels of beer to local pubs.

As an adolescent, Schultes was not very sociable, but he was driven to excel in his school work. He applied to only one college, Harvard, and was accepted. During his first year at college, he was on a tight budget. His money problems were eased when he received a Cudworth Scholarship, which provided tuition funds and a small stipend.

Schultes continued to work part-time for pocket money. He filed cards and shelved books at the Harvard Botanical Museum Library. The director, Oakes Ames, taught a course on practical botany and Schultes enrolled in the class during his third year of college. Ames was not a good lecturer and attracted few students. In fact, there were only five students in Schultes's class. The small class size meant that Ames could give personal attention to each student. He designed individual research projects that were equal to graduate-level assignments.

By chance, Schultes chose to study peyote, a small spineless cactus native to Mexico and the southwestern United States. Little was known about this plant at the time. Schultes soon discovered that the crown of the cactus—the only part that shows above ground—forms a small buttonlike structure. American Indians chew these "buttons" in some of their religious ceremonies and the cactus buttons cause hallucinatory visions. Schultes was fascinated by the idea that the little plants could have such a dramatic effect on the human mind. He decided to write his undergraduate thesis on peyote.

Ames indicated that Schultes needed to do field research before he could begin to organize his thesis. Therefore, the young man set out on a journey—financed by the independently wealthy Ames—to the American Southwest. In 1936, Schultes visited the Kiowa, one of the Indian tribes who used peyote, and observed the ceremonies where cactus buttons were a part of the ritual.

Peyote has been used in North and South America for untold centuries. In 1500s, when the Spaniards occupied Mexico, Catholic missionaries set out to convert the native population to Christianity. Later, members of the Inquisition—Spanish-organized, Catholic tribunals that disciplined disbelievers by captivity, punishment, or death—came to Mexico. Followers of the old Native American religions were severely punished, and the use of peyote was expressly forbidden. However, some of the tribes lived in isolated areas and old ways were preserved, protected from the Spanish priests and soldiers.

Years later, the U.S. government attempted to suppress the use of peyote in the religious ceremonies of the Native American Church—a recognized denomination in the United States. Indeed, anti-peyote laws were passed in nine states. In reaction to these restrictions, the use of peyote by Native Americans spread throughout the West and into Canada.

So it was that in the early summer of 1936, Dick Schultes and another young ethnobotanist, Weston La Barre, a graduate student from Yale, arrived in Oklahoma to explore the use of peyote by local Native Americans. Both young men were working under the direction of Alexander Lesser, a professor of anthropology at Columbia University. Lesser had arranged for Charlie Charcoal, a member of the Kiowa tribe, to join the group. The two students interviewed many tribal elders and eventually were admitted into a peyote ritual. Schultes's visions were limited to a succession of bright colors. When dawn came, he threw up violently but soon recovered. La Barre experienced more dramatic hallucinations. Although Schultes was somewhat disappointed in his experience, he developed a respect for the ceremony and later defended the use of peyote in several legal battles.

His next research subject was another mind-altering plant, the sacred mushroom of the Aztec. Some prominent botanists believed that stories of the mushroom were myths told by imaginative natives since the time of the conquistadores—the Spanish soldiers who conquered the Americas in the 1500s. However, Schultes, while working in the National Herbarium in Washington, D.C., had come across evidence that the stories were true. Dr. Ames was convinced that this student could find additional evidence in tropical Mexico and, again, Ames financed Schultes's research.

South of Mexico City and beyond the end of the railroad line, Schultes located the isolated villages of the Mazatec people. He soon verified the effects of the sacred mushrooms by observing a ceremony that combined religious visions, divination (predicting the future), and healing rituals. Schultes saw that the Mazatec's use of the mushroom closely paralleled the Plains Indians' use of peyote.

Schultes's next research project was conducted deep in the rain forests and concerned pre-Columbian practices of the Inca. He had located old references to a substance called by the Indian name *ololiuqui*. Prominent botanists believed that this plant was a relative of the thorn apple. Schultes thought otherwise. To him, the writings clearly showed that the plant was a climbing vine.

Schultes traveled by mule to the land of the Chinantec deep in the rain forests. In a small village, he visited the local healer and saw that his house was completely overgrown with a vine. Schultes learned that the seeds from this vine constituted the healer's sole medicine and that he sold the seeds to other shamans. The vine fit the Aztec description of *ololiuqui* in every detail. As Schultes had suspected, the historic plant was a vine of the morning glory family.

After his return to Harvard in the fall of 1939, Schultes worked on his doctoral dissertation and recuperated from an infection and the stresses of life in the jungle. He completed his dissertation and began a project sponsored by the Guggenheim Foundation. Schultes traveled back to the Amazon country to study the sources of arrow poisons used by the local peoples.

World of the Japanese attack on Pearl Harbor in Hawaii reached Schultes while he was staying in the Colombian town of Macoa. The attack caused the United States to enter World War II. Schultes immediately traveled to Bogotá to determine how he might help the war effort. However, the U.S. Embassy in Bogotá was in a confused state. After waiting two months for an assignment, Schultes returned to the Amazon area to continue his research on arrow poisons and other local plant-derived materials.

His progress was good. The young botanist identified a plant product used by the natives to cover wounds and lacerations. Known as "dragon's blood," the resin of the plant forms an antiseptic liquid bandage and the wounds heal with remarkable rapidity. Schultes also investigated a mood-altering substance called *yage*. This material is brewed as a tea from bark scrapings of a thick vine.

After his three-month survey of the recipes for arrow poison, Schultes returned to Bogotá. He had not yet received an official assignment from the U.S. government. Back into the rain forest he went—still under sponsorship of the

Richard Schultes in Brazil preparing botanical samples for preservation
(Courtesy of the Botanical Museum Library, Harvard University)

Guggenheim Foundation—and resumed work on his botanical surveys. This time, his journey took him into the lower
reaches of the Amazon, where wild rubber trees had once
been exploited for European markets.

World War II had disrupted the sources of many vital raw
materials. The great rubber plantations of Malaysia and
Indonesia were overrun by the Japanese at the start of the war.
The rubber situation became worse as the war progressed. The
development of synthetic rubber was incomplete, and the production of war materials required vast amounts of the material.
Recycling of worn-out tires and other sources supplied a small
fraction of the need. In desperation, officials of the U.S. government decided to try to reopen the wild rubber production of the
Amazon basin. They sought to identify the most productive wild
trees so that new plantations could be established in Puerto Rico
and the countries of Central America. Schultes and other
botanists were given the responsibility to identify the best stock
and collect seeds for new plantings. At last, Schultes had
received an official assignment from the government.

The botanists soon realized that a recurring blight could
attack and kill cultivated rubber trees. For this reason, only
wild species had been utilized in Brazil during the heyday of
the rubber boom. When the trees were cultivated in narrow
rows, the blight spread quickly from tree to tree and whole
plantations died out in one season. Wild trees were spaced far
enough apart so that one diseased tree would not automati-
cally infect the whole crop. Rubber trees in Malaysia were safe
because the spores of the blight were too fragile to survive the
long trip from the Amazon to East Asia.

For the next four years, Schultes worked on the problem of
cultivating rubber trees. Indeed, he continued his research after
World War II had drawn to a close. However, the venture was
never truly successful.

When Schultes returned to Harvard in 1953, he became
curator of the Orchid Herbarium at the Botanical Museum.

His early contributions to the field of botany included studies of peyote, the magic mushroom, the seeds of the morning glory, and the bark of the vine used to brew *yage*. Schultes brought careful scientific analysis to the investigation of mood-altering substances native to Central and South America.

During the 1960s and 1970s, while working with students at the herbarium, Schultes resumed his research on medicinal compounds. He and his students studied the role of coca leaves in the culture of the mountain Indians of South America. Schultes also began work on a compilation of medicinal plants of northwest Amazonia. Researchers estimate that there are as many as 80,000 species of plants in the Amazon jungles. Only a fraction of these species have been screened for various uses.

Schultes, his colleagues, and his students used the techniques of ethnobotany to identify 1,516 species of plants used by the native peoples of South America. Less than half of these plants have been scientifically evaluated. A book, *The Healing Forest*, was published in 1990 and contains descriptions and commentary on all 1,516 species. The volume is coauthored by Schultes and Robert Raffauf.

Freelance Exploring

Freelance explorers have contributed to the array of herbal medicines. The adventures of Nicole Maxwell provide an example of the independent scientist.

By her own account, Maxwell had a diversified educational background that included some medical training and some experience as a professional ballet dancer. She took up serious plant hunting in 1958 when she received a small grant from a major drug company. Maxwell explored the upper Amazon region for two years and made several interesting finds, including an herbal contraceptive.

When Maxwell returned to New York, her sponsors encouraged her to tell radio and television audiences about her exciting experiences as a plant hunter. However, the sponsors showed little interest in her plant discoveries. Possibly, the drug company did not want scientific interest in Maxwell's contraceptive to compete with the interest in their new, and similar, products. Perhaps early tests failed to show any effectiveness for the material. In fact, later studies suggest that the active ingredient in the contraceptive was provided by a microscopic fungus that infected the roots of the plant. The plant itself may have been totally ineffective.

Recently, the U.S. National Science Foundation (NSF) has begun a series of parallel programs that employ partnerships called International Cooperative Biodiversity Groups (ICBGs). Funds are drawn from the National Institutes of Health and the U.S. Agency for International Development as well as the NSF. The partnerships include members from universities, pharmaceutical companies, environmental organizations, and officials from the host countries. The goal of these partnerships is to find new drugs, stop the destruction of the rain forest, and provide employment for the forest people.

Five such groups are working toward this goal. One is in Suriname, a former Dutch colony on the northeastern coast of South America. The Suriname group is split into two teams. One team, from the Missouri Botanical Garden, is using conventional plant-finding techniques to secure medicinal plants for testing. They are collaborating with botanists from the Suriname National Herbarium. The other team is led by an ethnobotanist from Conservation International Suriname. This team has focused their efforts on medicinal plants that have been suggested by shamans. A Surinamese pharmaceutical company prepares extracts from these plants and ships the extracts to the United States for testing and analysis. David Kingston, a natural products chemistry professor at Virginia Polytechnical Institute who had worked on the development of taxol, was for some time the project director of the testing program. So far, about 30 of the 900 tested plants show some promise.

The sponsors of these projects have taken care to complete formal agreements with each host country. This will guarantee that governments, villagers, and other participants will receive a fair share in whatever benefits may arise. Great care is taken if a selected plant proves to have religious significance to any group involved with the project.

In addition, native shamans have been given permission to claim patent rights if plant materials used in their healing rituals are employed in any modern scientific preparation. Pharmaceutical companies are financing a variety of projects to improve the health and well-being of the forest peoples. These projects include bringing electricity into the villages and planning expanded development of forest products in addition to the herbal medicines. Conservation International, a nonprofit philanthropic organization, is taking steps to ensure the continuation of tribal traditions, rituals, healing methods, and history by recording the shamans as they discuss their practices.

In another move to protect native rights, the identity of the plants suggested by the shamans is not revealed unless the active ingredient is proven to be valuable. Then, the parties negotiate an arrangement for the utilization of the compound.

13

Testing for "Leads" and Beyond

When botanists, zoologists, and chemists talk about "leads," they are referring to natural materials that might yield extracts usable as medicines, foods, or other commercial products. In the search for new medicines, scientists know that the evidence of a biologically active material is the most valuable indicator of a lead. At the crudest level, bioactivity might be revealed by an intense odor, bitter taste, or by the evidence of a substance that can sicken or kill. Today, in addition to simple toxicity, field biologists use several other strategies to locate plants and animals that may be potential leads.

For example, ethnobiologists recognize that a natural material used as a traditional medicine or in religious rituals might be a lead. They also know that the traditional use of the lead may not be the best or only employment of the natural substance. Such was the case of vincristine, an extract from the rosy periwinkle plant. Folk healers use the extract to treat diabetes but extensive testing revealed that vincristine was not effective against diabetes but is an excellent treatment for some cancers.

Some field botanists use the study of taxonomy—the system by which plants and animals are classified—and their knowledge of plant heredity to search for leads. The investigation of the Solanaceae plant family is a good example of this method.

The family has at least 2,800 different species and includes many poisonous plants such as tobacco and foxglove. Therefore, plant hunters can study many possible leads from one large family. Marine biologists can use the same methods to identify possible animal leads. They know that marine animals without backbones, such as sponges, are notorious for poisons and therefore, may provide valuable medicines.

Those seeking potent natural products can also take an ecological approach and observe how plants and animals interact with each other. If a certain plant is strictly avoided by plant-eating animals, the avoidance may be caused by the unpleasant taste or smell that indicates a biologically active plant. Indeed, if oceanic predators avoid a particular soft coral, they are likely to have a good reason for their aversion.

Another approach to the search is more comprehensive and disciplined. Ethnobiologists select an area of a forest, lay out a grid in that space, and endeavor to obtain a sample of every organism that lives in the designated area. A diverse variety of plants and animals offer the hunters an increased likelihood of finding something valuable. The grid method can also be used underwater.

Another search strategy combines convenience and ease of collecting. Plant hunters sometimes confine their searches to areas alongside a newly finished road or a construction site. While this appears to be a lazy person's approach, such a method can be justified. Construction can upset the original plant and animal communities, and previously nonindigenous species are often introduced into the area. A similar strategy can lead the collector to a village marketplace where herbs and other plants are sold as folk medicines. This approach to ethnobiology allows the search to proceed without the hazards of trekking in areas of political unrest. For several years, plant hunters in Mexico have used such methods.

Once the plant, insect, or larger animal is collected, an initial extraction is performed. Usually the extract is derived from the leaves, bark, or roots of a plant; the entire body of an insect; or a single organ such as the skin or liver of a larger animal. Ideally, the first extraction is divided into two portions. One part is placed in test tubes containing water and the other in test tubes containing an oil solvent such as ether or alcohol. By testing for both water-soluble and oil-soluble materials, all the biologically active components of the sample will be captured.

Brine Shrimp Test

Brine shrimps are extraordinary creatures that are about the size of a small gnat and live in very salty water such as the Great Salt Lake in Utah. When environmental conditions are ideal, the females give birth to live offspring. When conditions are less than ideal, the female shrimps deposit eggs. Each of the eggs is encased in an extra-hard container called a cyst. Encysted, the tiny creatures are able to withstand adverse conditions such as cold or drought and can survive for months or years in a dormant state.

As often as three times a year, the cysts are harvested from the salty water and stored in freezers. The encysted shrimps are usually sold to pet stores as a food for tropical fish. Before being served as a fish food, the shrimps are immersed in warm water. The baby animals soon shed their cysts, feed on the available algae, and grow to 10 times their original size. The live shrimps thus provide a convenient, high-protein diet for tropical fish.

Drug developers, however, use the shrimps as an inexpensive screening tool in their search for leads. In one version of the brine shrimp test, a measured amount of distilled water and a specific number of live shrimps are placed in each of a set of— usually 30—test tubes. A predetermined amount of the extract being tested is added to the shrimps and water in each of the first set of 10 test tubes. In the next set of 10, the scientists add twice that amount of extract. No plant extract is placed in the last set of 10. The third set—which contains only shrimps and water—gives the researchers a base of comparison or what they call a "control." As an additional control, scientists usually use 10 identically filled test tubes for each dose level. This form of control provides a statistical check on the consistency of their procedures.

After 24 hours, the researchers count the living shrimps in each test tube. If the number of survivors in each tube is roughly the same, they know that the biological activity of the extract is low or nonexistent. If the high dose of extract kills almost all the shrimps, the lower dose kills about half the shrimps, and the set with no extract—the control—has few dead shrimps, the researchers know they have a promising lead.

Screening tests for the oil-soluble portion of an extract follow much the same procedure. "An oil soluble substance will form a film on the surface of the water in which mosquitos have hatched. Mosquito larvae must attach themselves to the surface in order to breathe. Consequently, the mosquitos are forced to come into contact with the test substance." If the oily substance is biologically active, the survival of the insect can be used in a manner parallel to the shrimp lethality test. Other tests use vulnerable young plants as the test subjects.

Poisons

In tests such as these, researchers equate the effects of a biologically active substance with the effects of a poison. Indeed, some scientists believe that the main difference between a medicine and a poison is the size of the dose. This approach to drug discovery has led researchers to investigate the manner in which poisons work on a single cell. At that level, poisons can affect the cell in one of four ways. One type of poison attacks the individual proteins that make up the cell membrane. Indeed, the poison can do irreparable harm by simply changing the shape of the proteins in some small way. Microbiologists now know that a protein's ability to function is determined by the manner in which each protein is folded or configured. If the fold is disturbed, the protein can no longer do its job.

A second type of poison adversely affects the efficiency of the pores in the cell membrane. The pores control the amount and kind of substances that enter into and exit from the cell. At the most basic level, cells take in or expel inorganic chemicals such as sodium, potassium, and calcium. More complicated exchanges take place in the transport of larger molecules such as sugars and amino acids. Many lethal poisons affect the transport of the simplest atoms, such as sodium, an element that is particularly important for muscle and nerve cells. Nerve cells cannot transmit their messages without the electrical energy provided by the sodium atoms.

Such messages are transmitted when tiny openings in the nerve cell membrane permit millions of sodium atoms to flow into the cell. This rapid intake occurs in a tiny fraction of a second and allows the creation of an electrical charge. Normally, the pores close when an adequate amount of sodium atoms have entered. Some substances act to hold the pores open after the cell's needs have been met. The oversupply of sodium causes the nerve cell to continue sending messages to the muscle cells. Soon the overstimulated muscles are subject to spasms and seizures. These muscle malfunctions are so severe that the heart and brain cannot function and the victim dies.

A third type of poison acts on the cell's reproductive system. The poisonous compound may penetrate the cell membrane and block a particular stage in the cell division sequence. This blockage might occur when the chromosomes are in the process of splitting into two sets. Even more dangerous, the poison might actually break up the DNA chain. This malfunction would set the stage for mutations and the death of the cell's offspring.

A fourth type of poison, one that has been discovered recently, jams the reproductive function of the cell by making it overproduce one or another cellular substructure. Such an overproduction seems to clutter the interior of the cell so that normal cell reproduction cannot take place.

These last two types of poisons are particularly important in cancer studies because these poisons interfere with cell reproduction. If the cells affected by the dysfunctional cell reproduction process could be specifically targeted, the cancer might be controlled without damaging normal, healthy cells.

Further Evaluation

The natural products chemist uses increasingly more complicated procedures to determine the true worth of a potential medicine. After the toxicity of an extract has been established, the next stage may require that living cells be brought into contact with the prospective drug. Great efforts are made to establish standard cell lines—cells cultivated for a specific purpose. Such special cells are used in cancer tests so that exacting comparisons can be made among the compounds being investigated. If further studies prove that the compound is not a potent anticancer drug, the compound may be tested as a possible antibiotic. In this case, pure strains of disease germs are used as the targets.

Instead of investigating the effectiveness of a single extract, some researchers save time and money by testing compounds that contain a mixture of incompletely refined animal or plant extracts. The initial tests on such a compound demonstrate whether the combination of extracts has any effect on cancer, the AIDS virus, or other targets of medical investigations. If the mixture has no effect on the chosen target, no attempt will be made to isolate or purify the component ingredients. Purification is hard work.

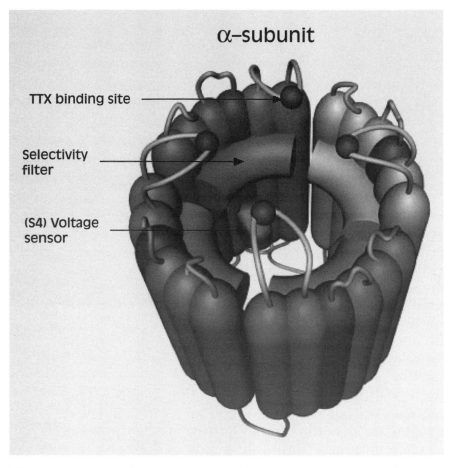

This diagram shows how the protein molecules are arranged as columns and hinges to make a channel to control the intake of sodium atoms by a nerve cell. (Courtesy of Tim Smith)

Fractional distillation is a method of purification that goes beyond simple solubility. If heating can vaporize the substance being studied, the vaporization can be partially controlled by increasing the temperature in predetermined stages. In this way, the component with the lowest boiling point is collected first and those with higher boiling points are collected as the temperature rises. This method of purification is never totally successful, however, because the vaporization of the component substances tends to overlap.

More sophisticated methods of separating components are based on chromatography. Botanists first used this technique to separate and study the different sizes of the dye molecules found in plants. In a more modern adaptation, uniformly sized grains of powder or very small pellets are poured into a glass column. This method allows the grains to be randomly but rather tightly spaced. The compound (usually diluted with a solvent) is then dripped into the column. The grains act as a filter to separate the different-sized molecules of the test compound. The largest molecules of the mixture are filtered out and captured by the powder near the top of the column. The smaller molecules trickle down and are filtered out at various stages of their descent. The smallest molecules settle to the bottom.

Chemists have invented many ways to separate the molecules in a mixture. Some methods—such as chromatography—are based on the size or mass of the molecule, some on the shape, and some on the responsiveness to an electrical charge. Once the ingredients in a mixture have been separated, the isolated substances can be identified by another set of tests.

Colorimetry is a relatively simple method of identification. In this technique, the unknown substance is mixed with a predetermined chemical. The specific color resulting from the mix identifies the unknown material. More sophisticated variations of this method use the technique of passing differing frequencies of light through an unknown substance. At each frequency, a measurement is made of the amount and intensity of light that has passed through the unknown material. Research has shown that each substance has a measurable and characteristic pattern when light is passed through it. Since such a pattern can be likened to a fingerprint, this method can identify the unknown by an analysis of the resultant pattern.

The assessment of biological activity has also been refined. Rather than testing the potential drug against whole, intact animal cells, special classes of molecules are now used as targets. Such molecules could be used in a study to investigate the proteins that bind materials to a cell's outer surface. The study might entail a series of tests to evaluate the effects of differing drug concentrations on differing types of binding proteins. Such multiple tests are often carried out simultaneously. The typical apparatus for these tests is a glass or plastic tray whose surface has rows of small, shallow depressions—usually 96 in number—to hold the materials being tested.

The required mixing, measuring, and depositing of these substances can be done by machine and requires only a small amount of time. However, the reactions do require time to be complete, and the tray is placed in an incubator for several hours. When the incubation is complete, the reaction is read— often by a machine. A tiny laser beam is aimed at each depression and the radiation emitted by the materials is measured. The level of radiation indicates whether binding reactions have taken place.

When a large set of simultaneous, computed-directed tests are carried out, the test procedures are known as "high throughput screening." This technique was developed and perfected during the race to unravel the human genome.

Crucial Tests for Drug Approval

The testing of new medicines is far from finished even after a chemist or pharmacologist has established that a new compound or mixture exhibits a set of desirable biological reactions. The next step is to ensure that the new material is reasonably safe for patients. In this phase, drug developers must administer various doses of the compound to test animals such as mice, hamsters, or white rats. Sometimes, these laboratory animals have been infected with the target disease or have been bred to be susceptible to a particular type of cancer.

If the new substance shows the desired effect on small animals, it will probably be tested on larger animals—perhaps on pigs. Scientists have found that pigs and humans have very similar biological systems. Because of this similarity, pigs are frequently used as test animals.

In the final stages, a new drug must be tested on human subjects for both safety and effectiveness. In the past, the last stages of testing were poorly regulated and drug developers often conducted such tests on themselves. For years, new drugs were also tested on subjects such as soldiers or prisoners. These people—most of whom had not volunteered their services—were unaware of the danger or purpose of the tests. Such experimental procedures are no longer allowed.

In the more recent past, practicing physicians were the main evaluators of a new drug. Drug companies provided doctors with samples of new drugs and gave appropriate warnings about the experimental status of the material. This practice was allowed because animal studies had shown that the compounds were not immediately lethal. A physician might administer the drug to carefully selected patients and keep records of the consequences. Such tests are no longer common. A more precise assessment of the safety and effectiveness of a new drug is now required by law. Such assessments are known as controlled clinical trials and are designed as rigorous experiments. Thoroughness is essential because the same drug can affect different people in quite dissimilar ways.

To minimize possible harm to human subjects, terminally ill patients are now asked to volunteer as test subjects. This may appear to be a cruel request, but many patients volunteer for such treatment in the hope that they might be helped or that their descendants might someday have access to a cure.

In order to achieve a definitive result from the tests, researchers must recruit a large number of test subjects. If possible, the subjects will be organized into groups according to age, gender, ethnicity, or some other variable. Research has shown that test results will be more precise if all the subjects in a particular test group share a similar characteristic.

The basic form of controlled clinical trial requires that the subject group be divided into three subgroups. Ideally, each subgroup will contain at least 20 subjects. One subgroup will be given the drug being evaluated. The second will be given a drug used as the current standard treatment for the target condition. The third subgroup will be given a placebo—the equivalent of an ineffective sugar pill. Neither the test subjects nor the test director are informed about which substance is being given to each subgroup. This technique is called the "double-blind" method and is a way to minimize prejudgments and maximize objectivity on the part of the experimenter and the subjects. To pass the initial clinical trials, the new drug must prove to be safe and more effective than the standard treatment. If the new drug exhibits such characteristics, additional tests will be warranted.

Subsequent tests will engage a larger number of subjects and may continue for years. U.S. Food and Drug Administration rules state that a new drug must be safe and effective before it can be approved. At this stage, the drug developer will have invested many thousands of dollars in the testing process. If and when approval is obtained, the developer faces the additional costs of manufacturing, promoting, and marketing the drug before any profits are achieved.

14
The National Institutes of Health

The National Institutes of Health (NIH) provide the research capabilities for the U.S. Department of Health and Human Services. The NIH grew out of the Public Health Service and gradually added research units that were focused on particular medical conditions. For example, the National Cancer Institute (NCI) was founded in 1937. Additional institutes were formed in 1945 immediately following the end of World War II. The increase in the number of units permitted the NIH to give attention to a full range of conditions such as infectious diseases and heart disease. Under the Public Health Service, the NIH now contains 23 institutes and centers and administered a budget of over $23 billion during the 2004 fiscal year.

Units Having Missions Related to Natural Sources

In the 21st century, three organizations within the NIH have a particular relevance to the search for natural sources of medicines. The largest of these was originally called the Office for Complementary and Alternative Medicine and is now known as the National Center for Complementary and Alternative

Medicine (NCCAM). This organization was formed at the urging of key senators and representatives and was founded by a law passed in 1991. At that time, the chair of the Senate Committee responsible for the NIH budget was a particularly strong advocate for the establishment of the new unit. Although senior scientists at the NIH were against the proposed organization, the new center was established by law in 1992.

The founding of NCCAM served several purposes. Alternative treatments, herbal compounds, and other dietary supplements had gained popularity and widespread usage. Large surveys show that more than 40 percent of the U.S. population use vitamin supplements regularly and at least 14 percent use herbal supplements. Elected officials realized that their support of the new legislation could be translated into many potential votes.

At the time that this legislation was introduced, many users of alternative remedies were distressed because the costs of alternative therapies and dietary supplements were—and still are—rarely reimbursed by any kind of health-care insurance. Many citizens wanted actions that would change the status of such treatments. The establishment of a research facility to test the treatments in an acceptable scientific manner might help overcome one of the barriers to reimbursement. This type of research was clearly within the mandate of the NIH.

The scientific testing of complementary and alternative health-care materials and practices would also help defend these methods from their critics. Indeed, some officials in government agencies—such as the U.S. Food and Drug Administration (FDA)—were seen as antagonists who wanted to restrict access to untested drugs and treatments. Television, newspapers, and magazines carried news items questioning the safety and effectiveness of complementary and alternative health-care products. The manufacturers and distributors of these materials became worried about the reputations of their products. The companies joined together to lobby for new legislation that would help establish the legitimacy of their herbal supplements and other alterative health-care products.

Lastly, even the opponents of the legislation agreed that the information accumulated from the scientific study of alternative treatments and dietary supplements would help physicians and other care providers take into account the effects of patients' self-medication using such treatments and supplements. Conventional treatment programs could then be planned so that the conventional and the nonconventional treatments would not interfere with each other.

Scientists in the new center first planned to conduct reviews of the existing research on each dietary supplement or technique. They hoped to confirm (or disconfirm) the idea that the procedures and supplements were supportive of good health. However, it soon became clear that very little high-quality research was available to be reviewed. As NCCAM became better organized, staff members initiated new research projects that would help gain the necessary information. In addition, research grants were awarded to outside scientists at major medical schools and other institutions. In 2003, NCCAM was overseeing 172 research projects. Some 54 of these studies were designed to evaluate popular herbal materials. These evaluations included comparing the effects of herbal remedies against those of conventional medicines. Researchers also assessed the side effects or negative aspects of using nontraditional medicines to treat a specific category of patients, such as pregnant women or AIDS patients.

Saint-John's-wort—a popular herbal material used to control depression—was one of the nontraditional substances tested by NCCAM. In a controlled clinical trial, the effects of Saint-John's-wort were compared with those of a standard antidepressant and a placebo (a sugar pill that has no effect on the body and is used in comparing the effects of various medications). The results, published in 2002, showed that neither the antidepressant medication nor the herbal remedy made from Saint-John's-wort was more effective than the placebo. After these findings, the researchers suggested that the herb be tested against other antidepressants to obtain a complete picture of its worth as a health aid. Additional clinical trials indicated that Saint-John's-wort might interfere with the action of some drugs used to treat HIV infections. AIDS patients were warned to stop using that herbal compound.

In addition to such targeted research efforts, financial backing was provided for 21 research centers with relatively broad charters that allow flexible research programs. With an annual budget of just over $115 million, each project and each research center could be given only limited support. Nevertheless, the establishment of NCCAM within the National Institutes of Health signifies a serious attempt to overcome the uncertainties and ambiguities associated with nonconventional health care.

The Office of Dietary Supplements

In 1994, members of the House of Representatives introduced an amendment to the Food, Drug and Cosmetic Act that addressed the issue of providing the public with pertinent information about dietary supplements. A task force discussed the amount and type of information that needed to be included on the labels of such products. The law's proponents and the task force members recognized that the composition, safety, and effectiveness of the products had not been well researched. Therefore, many of their questions about the labeling of dietary supplements could not be answered. As a short-term solution to the problem, members of Congress asked that specialists at the NIH be given the task of systematizing the existing knowledge, coordinating attempts to answer specific questions, and expanding the knowledge base. Consequently a small team was assembled and designated as the Office of Dietary Supplements. This group works directly under the director of NIH. Their work includes the provision of exchanging findings among specialists and communicating information on dietary supplements to the public.

The Natural Products Branch

The Natural Products Branch of the National Cancer Institute (NCI) is the third group within the NIH that is involved with natural medicines. This unit has the responsibility for seeking plant and animal sources of medicines and screening these sources for their curative or ameliorative properties. The Natural Products Branch is a main source of support and encouragement for present-day plant hunters.

Many modern plant hunters are affiliated with herbariums, arboretums, or botanical gardens and are trained in the botanical sciences. Others are affiliated with colleges and universities. Many of these academics, who hold degrees in anthropology, refer to themselves as ethnobotanists. Large pharmaceutical companies employ members of a third group of plant hunters. Most have been trained in organic chemistry or in pharmacology. To some degree, modern plant hunters must have a combination of skills and knowledge of all the pertinent disciplines—anthropology, botany, chemistry, and pharmacology.

A fourth group of plant hunters is composed of the official field botanists of the U.S. Department of Agriculture (USDA). The USDA began its program in field botany in 1898. The directors sent their first expedition to Russia with the goal of finding superior crop plants and arranging for their exportation to the United States. The pioneer plant hunter and agronomist Mark A. Carleton led the mission. His expedition was a success, and Carleton brought back hardy strains of wheat from Russia and new strains of oats and barley from Scandinavia. Soon, the new plants were introduced to American farmers. The botanists who followed Carleton as field workers for the USDA sought additional nonnative plants that could be adopted by farmers. At that time, medicinal plants were of secondary interest. After the end of World War II in 1945, however, priorities began to change. By the 1950s, economic botany emerged as a new subspecialty of agronomy. Proponents of the new discipline had recognized the similarity of methods and goals among field workers seeking food plants, those seeking ornamental plants for flower gardens, and those seeking medicinal plants. Leaders of botanical science urged the plant hunters to join a common organization, and in 1959, the Society for Economic Botany was formed.

In the early 1960s, the NCI began initiating agreements with organizations that undertook research expeditions to gain further knowledge in the field of economic botany. Although universities, pharmaceutical firms, and major botanical gardens all played important roles, the major partner was the USDA. The development of taxol, a leading anticancer drug, is an example of this partnership.

Under the direction of the NCI, many thousands of plant specimens were collected and screened for biological effects between 1961 and 1981. Unfortunately, only a small number passed the elementary screening. The lack of success led to a temporary cessation of specimen collection between 1981 and 1985. However, new methods of rapid screening became available after the mid-1980s, and new research allowed a deeper understanding of the biological activities of anticancer materials. These advancements encouraged a resumption of the collection process. In 2004, almost 250 lead compounds—plant and animal materials that have a reasonable probability of being future sources of medicine—were being studied and assessed. The renewed interest can also be seen at an NCI facility in Frederick, Maryland, where several thousand specimens of source materials are stored for future examination.

Antibiotics against Cancer

Of the 250 lead compounds being studied, about 60 are from microorganisms such as molds and fungi. In some cases, these compounds have been prescreened and found to be effective as antibiotics. Compounds that have proven to be effective antibiotics are of special interest to biomedical researchers. These scientists hold the idea is that if a compound can kill a bacterium, it might also be able to kill a cancer cell.

One such antibiotic was discovered in 1943 when a seven-year-old girl named Margaret Tracy was brought to Presbyterian Hospital in New York City. An emergency room resident treated the girl for an infected wound that would not heal. The resident wanted to know the exact bacterium that was causing the problem and sent a sample from the wound to the laboratory. There, a bacteriologist named Babina Johnson examined the material under a microscope. She noted the appearance of two different strains of infectious microbes, *Staphylococcus auras* and *Bacillus subtilis*. Johnson wanted the colonies to multiply so she could make sure of their identities. She placed a sample of the infected material in a shallow plate called a Petri dish. The dish was loaded with agar a gelatin-like material that fostered the growth of microorganisms. In the morning, the *Bacillus subtilis* was prospering but the *Staphylococci* were all gone. She reported her observations to Dr. Frank Meleney, and they deduced that the *Bacillus subtilis* was producing a substance that killed the other microbes. They collaborated in isolating and purifying the substance, verified its antibiotic effects, and named it Bacitracin. The name of the new medicine is a combination of *Bacillus subtilis*—the source microbe—and Tracy, the last name of the girl from whom the microbe had been recovered. Bacitracin is now used extensively as a topical (exterior) wound dressing but because of its toxicity cannot be injected like penicillin. However, it is among the antibiotics being tested for activity against cancers.

Animal Sources

Although many plants have been identified as possible sources of antibiotic or anticancer compounds, only a few animals have been recognized as potential sources of medicine. One is the large African frog, *Xenopus laevis,* and its cousin, *Xenopus tropicalis.* Xenopus has long been a favorite of biology teachers because of its rapid growth from egg to adult.

Continuing research on *Xenopus* has shown that the frog eggs produce protective chemicals. One such chemical, Tetrocarcin-A, has become important to cancer researchers. Tetrocarcin-A does not directly attack cancer cells but reduces a cancer cell's ability to defend itself from other anticancer drugs. The new drug thus allows the anticancer drug to do its job. Scientists at the FDA have not yet approved Tetrocarcin-A for

Xenopus laevis *is a large frog of African origin that is useful to biologists in many ways.* (Courtesy of the National Science Foundation)

regular treatments, but its acceptance is being pursued.

Toxicity is a characteristic of many of the exotic compounds being tested for use against cancer. Several animals and many insects produce poisonous secretions for defensive purposes. Because of its toxicity, the blister beetle is of particular interest to the NCI. One species of blister beetle has a long history of use as a folk aphrodisiac—or love potion—called Spanish fly. To make the aphrodisiac, the wings of the insect are crushed into a powder. The powder is then mixed with a liquid and drunk. The effectiveness of the blister beetle as an aphrodisiac is highly debatable. Today, scientists are interested in the

There are many types of blister beetles. This is the striped variety. (Courtesy of the horticulture department, Texas A&M University)

possibility that two types of blister beetle secretions may prove effective as components of anticancer drugs. Both are extremely poisonous in purified form and a lethal dose is smaller than a single drop. One of these poisons is water-soluble and contains as many as 50 different alkaloids. The most prevalent of these alkaloids is called cantharidin and has been shown to kill cancer cells in the laboratory. A second is an oily secretion that comes from a subspecies of blister beetle. Its main constituent, called harmonine, can also kill cancer cells. Scientists are studying ways to reduce the harmful side effects of cantharidin and harmonine so that these drugs can receive approval from the FDA.

This is one variety of soft coral called a fan coral. (Courtesy of Ria Tan, Singapore)

Research is also underway on compounds from several types of sea creatures. Coral is of special interest to drug developers because it is relatively easy to harvest. Coral is now a popular dietary supplement and regarded by some as a prime source of dietary calcium. However, there is considerable doubt that coral calcium is any better than calcium from other sources. In any case, biomedical researchers have little interest in coral as a source of dietary calcium. Their interest lies in investigating the organic chemicals produced by corals as defenses against predators such as starfish.

Although a study of crassin, a defensive chemical produced by soft Caribbean coral, has revealed some antibiotic effects, two other soft coral candidates seem to have more potential. One is called eleutherobin and comes from a soft coral living off the coast of Australia. A second, sarcodictyin, is from a type of Mediterranean coral. The anticancer and antibiotic effects of both corals are being investigated.

The soft corals are as immobile as their commonplace, rock-like cousins, but unlike their cousins they are relatively scarce. Furthermore, some countries have put severe restrictions on harvesting these creatures. Such prohibitions, combined with a natural scarcity, have encouraged chemists to develop synthetic versions of the soft corals' defensive chemicals. The scientists at the Scripps Research Institute in southern California developed such synthetic chemicals in 1998. They are now experimenting with variations of these molecules to develop a drug with fewer toxic side effects.

Tunicates are soft-bodied sea creatures that sometimes look like colorful, small balloons. Unlike corals, they are mobile (although definitely not speedy). Scientists have found that one species of tunicate produces a promising substance called didemnin, a chemical with multiple biological effects. Didemnin can act against some viruses as well as attack the cancer cells of leukemia. One form of this drug has passed a second series of clinical trials that will determine its effectiveness. However, it is considered too dangerous for routine use.

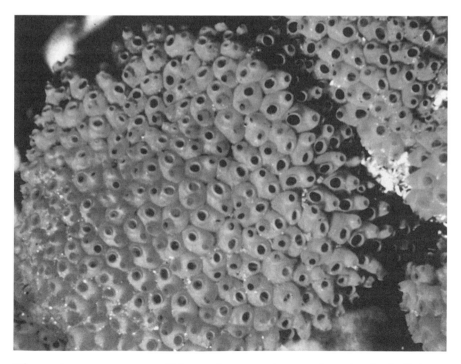

The tunicate can move swiftly on the ocean bottom by using its built-in water jet. (Courtesy Ria Tan, Singapore)

Similar chemicals from other tunicates may have less toxicity and, at present, are under clinical test.

Scientists long suspected sponges of harboring potent, anticancer compounds. In the 1990s, research programs of the NCI succeeded in identifying a promising compound called discodermolide. In 1998, a license to develop discodermolide was offered to a European pharmaceutical company by officials of the NCI. Early laboratory tests indicated that the drug was effective against cancers that were otherwise resistant to chemical treatments. Because these preliminary tests looked so promising, the officials hoped to shorten the time between those tests and the more rigorous clinical trials. Unfortunately, the appropriate, deepwater sponges are difficult to locate and harvest because divers can stay underwater for only relatively short periods of time. Also, the amount of the active chemical in each animal is miniscule and a large number of sponges must be gathered to investigate the value of discodermolide. Therefore, the progress toward clinical trials has been slow. Attempts to synthesize this potentially valuable compound have also proven difficult and time-consuming. At present, the company is trying to construct similar molecules to those of discodermolide.

Bryostatin is one of the most promising of the other lead chemicals derived from ocean creatures. This compound comes from an animal that fouls the hulls of ships, dock pilings, and any other solid object in the water. The creatures are called "moss

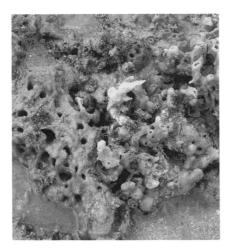

These deepwater sponges grow in diversified colonies. (Courtesy of Ria Tan, Singapore)

animals" because they spread their bodies in a sheetlike pattern over whatever object they occupy. Harvesting these animals would serve to clean up harbor areas and support the production of a drug that appears to be effective against some forms of skin cancer—a win-win outcome.

Plant Sources

Of the more than 200 lead chemicals under study by the NCI, there are dozens that come from plant sources. Some examples are worth describing in detail. At the top of the list is camptothecin, a chemical long used as a traditional Chinese medicine. The medicine is made from the bark and leaves of *Camptotheca acuminata*—a tree native to an area in subtropical China. The tree's reputation as a cure for many maladies led to its name, which is translated as "Happy Tree." USDA explorers traveled to China to collect its seeds and seedlings as early as 1911. At that time, the collectors were mainly interested in using the tree as an ornamental shade tree. *Camptotheca*, which is related to the black gum tree found in the southern United States, grows rapidly in a mild climate and reaches a mature height of about 25 feet. By 1927, many shipments of "Happy Tree" had been received by botanical gardens throughout the United States. In 1950, as scientists became more interested in investigating plants with a history of medicinal usage, researchers began collecting samples of bark and leaves of the tree for use in pharmacological tests. The samples were studied as a prospective source of raw materials for the fabrication of female sex hormones that have several medical uses, including contraception. Investigation did not support that possibility but additional study revealed a wide range of biologically active compounds. Biochemists under contract to the NCI found that chemicals from the bark and leaves killed a variety of cancer cells, but further research

The "Happy Tree" is native to China but grows now as a shade tree in many parts of the world. Now that extracts are used against cancer, it is even more valuable.
(Courtesy of James Manhart, Texas A&M University)

showed that the pure extracts were too toxic for regular use. However, biochemists have been able to build less-toxic, synthetic molecules that follow the main pattern of the natural substance. Several of these offspring drugs have been approved by the FDA and are in regular use.

Poisonous plants are often of special interest to biomedical scientists in their search to control cancer. One such plant is the rattlebox, a weed that grows in fallow fields and sometimes in pastures. If eaten by farm animals, the weed can be fatal. Researchers found that the key ingredient, monocrotaline, tends to attack liver cells and smooth muscle cells in the heart and lungs. Ironically, it also attacks the cancer cells that grow in these organs. Scientists are working to construct a synthetic version of monocrotaline that will be less toxic but equally effective against cancer.

Another profoundly poisonous plant is the jimsonweed (*Datura stramonium*), a species that may have originated in Mexico. Historical records reveal that Native Americans both south and north of Mexico used the plants to make a hallucinogenic for religious ceremonies. Today, native healers use tinctures made from the plant as a medicine to heal wounds and as a painkiller.

The name of the plant is derived from events that occurred at a British garrison in colonial Jamestown. Some of the soldiers thought that the leaves of the plant could be cooked as greens and eaten as a side dish. When several died as a consequence, the deadly plant became known as the Jamestown weed—later shortened to jimsonweed. The jimsonweed plant produces beautiful white or pink flowers that mature into seedpods that are round and covered with thorns. Because of this feature, the plant is also known as the thorn apple. Jimsonweed is of the family Solanaceae, which includes tobacco, tomatoes, and potatoes. Many family members of Solanaceae are poisonous.

The principle bioactive chemical in jimsonweed is called stramonium and is a mixture of alkaloids. Ironically, stramonium is used as a control agent for cancer of the brain and central nervous system. Thus, the negative effects that stramonium causes on the central nervous system—hallucinations and loss of consciousness—is balanced by the positive effect of halting cancers in the same organs.

Parthenolide, an anticancer substance derived from the wildflower feverfew, is far less toxic than stramonium. Feverfew is a member of the daisy/aster family, and a domestic variety of feverfew is known to gardeners as bachelor's buttons. For many years, dried and powdered feverfew leaves have been used as a folk remedy. Like aspirin, it acts as

The rattlebox is a pasture weed that is a member of the pea family. Cattle and other livestock must avoid it because it is poisonous. (Courtesy of Jochen Wagner)

The jimsonweed is a member of a family of plants that contains many poisonous species. (Courtesy of Kevin McGuire)

an anti-inflammatory and reduces the pain of migraine headaches. Biomedical researchers have established that parthenolide does not directly attack cancer cells but improves the anticancer actions of other established drugs.

Today the agencies of the NIH continue to have a strong interest in natural substances as possible sources of new medicines. Most of the initial research was confined to identifying possible treatments for cancer. Over the past several years, research programs have broadened to include the search for medications to fight HIV/AIDS. Scientists at the NIH are also investigating folk remedies and herbal supplements that can be used to augment or replace conventional medicines in the treatment of diseases other than cancer and HIV/AIDS.

Global Developments

Serious differences exist among nations with respect to their rules governing the use of natural medicines. Some of these differences are the result of variations in scientific infrastructures and are mainly related to relative economic conditions. However, differences still exist among the most technically advanced societies. For example, herbal compounds are more often used by German physicians than by American doctors.

Administrators at the World Health Organization (WHO) see these discrepancies as a problem. For one thing, the differences in outlook can impair the cooperation between health-care providers in third-country settings. Consequently, in 2004, a major project directed toward a unification of views about natural products was mounted by the leaders of WHO. American medical scientists see this move as a constructive response to the establishment of the National Center for Complementary and Alternative Medicine in the NIH.

Feverfew has been used in folk medicine for hundreds of years. (Courtesy of Linda Dodge)

15

Searching for Natural Materials in the 21st Century

The plant hunters of the 17th, 18th, and 19th centuries usually sought permission from government officials to search for exotic and interesting plants in the tropical hunting grounds in Asia, Africa, and South America. These naturalists often represented their own governments and were freely accepted as guests of the host countries. Although a small minority exploited their freedom of movement, the official hosts rarely considered the botanical scholars a threat to national integrity. Indeed, the plant hunters' activities caused little or no fanfare, and they seldom became involved with the local people.

During the first half of the 20th century, those ethnobotanists who were studying the people of tropical lands became increasingly interested in the ways that healers and ceremonial leaders used local plants and their extracts. Outside of the academic communities, however, few people knew or cared about these activities. Gradually, after the 1950s, plant hunting became a far more visible exercise. Soon, local politicians demanded restrictions on the investigations of the ethnobotanists. This change in position was driven by many factors. One was the decline of colonialism. Although the countries of Latin America had achieved independence about 100 years earlier, countries in Asia and Africa were then being freed from their colonial rulers and emerging as newly independent nations. Local political leaders were now able to establish rules that governed the conduct of foreign visitors. The leaders wanted to advance the financial status and well-being of their own people rather than allow foreigners to take advantage of untapped resources. They realized that some foreign visitors were uninterested in the welfare of the local population and sought only their own financial gain.

As these leaders gained a voice in international affairs, the world learned of the widespread impoverishment of the people in many newly independent nations. Spokespeople for the industrialized countries advanced a variety of plans to improve local economic conditions in the poorer countries. In the 1970s, concerned officials sought to provide technical support for developing village-level production centers. In one program, village leaders were given tools to fabricate containers from locally grown fibers. The containers were then used for transporting the village's agricultural produce to market centers. Thus, the tools were a source of multiple benefits—the growth of skills, the production of a needed article, and the means to transport and sell local commodities. Advocates of such programs adopted the slogan "Small Is Beautiful."

Although such programs were beneficial to the local inhabitants, scholars and activists were concerned that the loss of native culture could result from the modernization efforts of outsiders. Plant scientists and others were also worried about the destruction of ecosystems and the extinction of species as the tropical forests were harvested for timber and medicinal plants.

The Convention on Biodiversity

These and related issues came to a head in 1992. In that year, the United Nations Environment Programme hosted a major conference in Rio de Janeiro, Brazil. Many aspects of environmental protection were addressed, but the loss of tropical ecosystems was prominent in the minds of many attendees. The theme adopted by the assembled delegates was the preservation of biodiversity. The delegates at the convention argued that harvesting the tropical forests meant that some plant and animal communities would be destroyed and that species that might have shown medical potential would be lost forever.

The delegates were instructed to draw up a "convention" that could serve as a contractual agreement or treaty among all the countries. Governmental officials were asked to resist any agreements that would result in the destruction of their forests. The document further stated that the native, forest-dwelling people would be given the major responsibility for preserving their home areas. In effect, indigenous people were made the stewards of the forest and its resources. They were to be consulted about any forest research studies and involved in all decisions about forest usage. Logging and mining companies were seen to be the most dangerous outsiders, but plant hunters could not be overlooked as potential exploiters of forest assets. The provisions laid down by the convention transformed the activities of plant hunters and ethnologists from unobtrusive and private undertakings to unavoidably visible and politically provocative ventures.

Bioprospecting

Bioprospecting is the new name given to the activity of hunting for natural sources of potentially valuable chemicals. In the decades before 1992, commercial drug manufacturers rarely sent plant hunters into the tropical forests. However, the discovery of the vinca alkaloids, from rosy periwinkle and taxol, from the Pacific yew, had enlivened their interest in botanical exploration. Although neither of those were specifically tropical plants, scientists knew that the tropics supported the largest variety of plant species in the world and that this great variety could provide some valuable chemicals.

Soon, new types of arrangements were needed to expedite the work of the plant hunters. Officials of five types of organizations involved in botanical exploration established contractual agreements. The most important of these were the relevant government agency in the sponsoring country and its counterpart in the host country. An agreement between these two was essential to the commencement of bioprospecting.

The cooperation of academic institutions in the two countries was also vital to the search for natural raw materials. The hunt managers were often faculty members of an institution in the sponsoring country. A university in the host country might provide the expert botanists or chemists who would conduct the actual explorations. The host country institution also might offer the foreign scholars temporary positions on the teaching faculty or perhaps full use of the university facilities.

Finally, the fifth type of participant was a pharmaceutical firm—sometimes more than one—willing to help finance the expeditions. Usually, all the participating organizations were linked by contracts but sometimes only by a recognition of mutual interests and a "gentleman's agreement."

Often left out of this formal network were the native peoples who dwelt in the tropical forests. In a few cases, the indigenous people were organized—such as in tribal councils—and could participate in contractual commitments. However, in most cases, high-level government officials from both countries and executives of the participating drug companies held the responsibility to abide by the United Nations convention and ensure fair treatment for the locals. In other words, the high-level guests and their equally high-level hosts could determine what would be done for the indigenous people.

The favorite method of dealing with the locals was to pay a modest fee to enter and explore the desired lands. This payment was coupled with the promise of royalties from marketing any medicines derived from local plants. Since most medicines from natural sources require a 10- to 12-year period to develop and market the product, royalty sharing was a distant goal for the indigenous people. Some of the local inhabitants were also unhappy about the promised entrance fees. Instead of badly needed cash, they were often provided with goods and services such as classroom teachers or crates of tools. Most of these goods and services were badly needed but some were unwanted or unhelpful.

Many of the bioprospectors saw a need to improve their rapport with the native people. Sponsors and scientists encouraged the locals to consider the explorations as joint ventures and invited them to work alongside the ethnobotanists. The plant hunters hoped that this effort would give the indigenous people a sense of part ownership in the enterprise and contribute to its success. The forest dwellers responded by sharing their knowledge of local plants and animals. They also pointed out prospective sources of medicinal compounds, such as the plants used in traditional healing.

Sometimes the joint ventures had little connection with the search for medicinal plants. In one case, the sponsors purchased plumbing equipment and joined with the native workers to install new, modern bathrooms in the local school building. In this and similar undertakings, the visitors had chosen the approach established earlier by Peace Corps volunteers and similar nongovernmental organizations.

The expedition leaders wanted to believe that these joint ventures were beneficial to both the visiting scientists and the native people. However, the visitors also recognized that such cooperative efforts were difficult to advance. In some instances, the problem arose from long-lasting rifts between the locals and their own government. In some cases, the impoverished locals were actually engaged in a form of low-level warfare against the central government. Some of their anger and mistrust was also directed toward the members of the scientific expeditions. The academic botanists became aware that working among a people who were involved in local, antigovernment uprisings did not support a healthy or productive work environment.

The Hoodia and the San People

The case of the hoodia and the San illustrates other problems encountered during the modern search for natural medicines. The hoodia is a desert plant with an upright stalk that is about the size and shape of a large cucumber laced with sharp spines. In season, the cactus-like species has dusty, pink flowers at the top of its stems.

The San, a desert people of the Kalahari, are sometimes known as "Bushmen." They have several distinct sub-groupings, the largest of which speaks a language that employs clicks as one form of articulation. The San are semi-migratory—small groups build settlements, remain for a season, and then move to new grounds when the season changes. Specifically, they live in the desert during the wet or rainy months and move to the fringe of the desert with the arrival of the dry season. The men of the group typically hunt wild game and the women gather vegetable foods. The

The hoodia plant resembles a cactus but comes from another botanical family. (Courtesy of Lytton Musselman)

hunting expeditions can last for several days and the San men are exposed to desert conditions such as the scarcity or total unavailability of food or water. During these treks, the San use the hoodia to alleviate hunger and thirst. They strip off the thorns, cut slices from the stem, and chew the bitter pulp. The plant has an extraordinary power to reduce hunger and thirst.

Aware of the hoodia's unusual properties, botanical surveys were organized by plant hunters from the Council for Scientific Research, an agency of the government of the Union of South Africa. Bioprospectors located the hoodia and laboratory workers extracted the plants' soluble compounds to isolate and study the active ingredient. The government of the Union of South Africa licensed the compound to Phytopharm, a small pharmaceutical company based in England. Phytopharm, in turn, licensed it to Pfizer, a major American firm. Pfizer would do the clinical tests and marketing.

The rights of the San people were completely ignored while these transactions were going forward. When questioned by advocates for the rights of indigenous peoples, the South African government asserted that the San were extinct. This was incorrect. The San had scattered into the areas surrounding the Kalahari Desert. These migrations had occurred because the ecology of the desert was changing and game was becoming scarce. To gain a livelihood, some of the San were working as unskilled laborers in the small cities that border the desert. Although these people were not extinct, the San's dispersal from their native lands may have made them difficult to locate—especially if those who sought the San were not eager to find them.

Representatives of the dispersed groups were finally drawn together by indigenous leaders and human rights advocates. The San ultimately formed a legally recognized cooperative, the Working Group of Indigenous Minorities in South Africa (WIMSA). These native people could now carry out negotiations with the South African government, the English company, and the American pharmaceutical firm.

After the first year of a three-year negotiation period, the San were granted the intellectual property rights to the hoodia plant. Their millennium-long tradition of using the plant and their knowledge of its properties established their right to this legally accepted concept. Agreements about sharing any benefits from the marketing of hoodia derivatives could now go forward. In 2003, all the interested parties, including the San, were able to reach a detailed agreement about profit sharing and the equal treatment of all parties.

Research on the hoodia plant had begun when apartheid was still the law in South Africa. When native peoples took over the government, the laws governing fair and equal treatment for all peoples were established, and these regulations were followed by the commercial companies. The agreement reached during negotiations with the San and the other participants reinforced the laws of the new South African government.

The San, a people with strong traditions of agreeability and consensus, had no intention of disrupting the progress of deriving a salable commodity from the hoodia plant. They recognized that this process would require years of effort and were willing to be patient.

The Neem Tree

The neem is native to India. The mature tree yields many seeds, and young trees tend to grow up in various uncultivated locations such as roadsides. The neem is in the same family as mahogany and closely related to a tree that is common in the southern United States called the Chinaberry tree (or sometimes, the umbrella tree). The local villagers in central India use every part of the neem for a host of health care and other applications. Extracts of the bark and leaves are used as insecticides

Neem trees growing in the African country of Mali (Courtesy of the U.S. Agency for International Development)

and fungicides. Neem twigs are used as toothbrushes. A pulp from the fruit is used as soap with possible germicidal properties. Resin from the bark is used as glue.

In the 1920s, chemists began to study the neem. The main focus at the time was the possible commercial application as a pesticide. In the 1980s, journalists began to publicize the tree as a cornucopia of health-giving products. Product engineers at major industrial firms became interested and worked on ways in which the raw material could be processed into a marketable pesticide product. In 1990, the W. R. Grace Company filed for patents in the United States and Europe on the use of an extract of the neem seeds as a pesticide.

When the patent application was publicized, a storm of protest began on the part of groups trying to protect the rights of the local villagers. The protesters contended that a company should not be able to patent a plant. There was fear expressed that the villagers might have to pay a fee to use a plant that had been freely available to them for generations. When elements of the government of India stepped into the legal battle, the patent application was withdrawn. Patent protection for a particular use of a compound, no matter how unique the compound, is not often allowed. The natives had used extracts of the neem seeds as pesticides for years, so the use was not novel in any case.

In the wake of the tempest, many patents have, in fact, been awarded for the exploitation of parts of the neem. These patents cover the technical procedures for the extraction of critical ingredients and their preservation during storage and transportation. Product designers have also suggested additional commercial uses such as antitumor medicine and contraception. Most of the present patent holders and new applicants now realize that they should compensate the local people to avoid a stonewall of opposition to their efforts.

Neem trees grow rapidly and are ideal as shade trees. (Courtesy of the U.S. National Park Service)

Other Examples

From a global perspective, the end of the 20th century and the beginning of the 21st century was a time of commercial initiatives for bioprospectors.

Pharmaceutical companies, both large and small, were sponsoring their own private expeditions on the high seas and on dry land.

The Puffer Fish

The puffer fish, well-known as a dangerous delicacy offered by some sushi restaurants, offered an attractive target to plant and animal hunters. The fish is harvested from the ocean in fairly large numbers and its toxic organs discarded by the fishing industry. Thus, for little cash outlay, a drug company could acquire the raw material by recovering the discarded waste. Unfortunately even tiny doses of the purified substance, tetrodotoxin, proved lethal. Tetrodotoxin and similar poisons act on the sodium channels in cell membranes. These channels regulate the amount of sodium that enters a cell. Some poisons hold the channels open and allow too much sodium to enter. This overabundance leads to violent and often lethal spasms. Tetrodotoxin, on the other hand, plugs the channels so that not enough sodium enters the cell. If a nerve cell has received too little sodium, it will fail to transmit any pain signals. Therefore, the drug companies decided that tetrodotoxin had potential use as a painkiller and tried some structural modifications of

The puffer fish is relished in the preparation of sushi, thin strips of raw fish rolled with other ingredients such as herbs and spices. However, if not prepared properly, it can poison the consumer.
(Courtesy of Jim Christensen)

the poison molecule. The tests of one such modification suggested a totally unimagined use for the poison. The substance seems to act as a soothing remedy for drug addicts. The pain and discomfort of the withdrawal process appear to be diminished by the modified molecule. Further testing is needed before approval by the U.S. Food and Drug Administration.

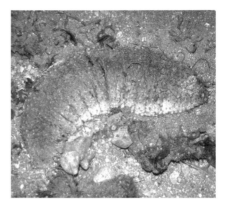

The sea cucumber is regarded by some as a food delicacy. Researches believe that it might also produce medicinal chemicals. (Courtesy of Ria Tan, Singapore)

Other Sea Creatures

Investigations of other sea creatures have included the search for a species of shallow water sponges native to the west coast of Australia. However, the regional government has banned the exploration. Local officials contend that such activities might cause the extinction of the sponges and provide no compensation for the local government.

Because of the relatively small number of scientists engaged as bioprospectors, only a few of the thousands of aquatic animals have been studied for their potential, medicinal properties. However, the situation may be improving because pharmaceutical companies are financing more research. University scientists in England are launching a study of the chemicals in starfish eggs. Other studies have been initiated by commercial firms to determine whether dried sea cucumber, often prescribed as a remedy by traditional Chinese healers, may provide a lead to new drugs. Even sea worms are candidates for medicine production.

More Plant Sources

University scientists under contract to commercial firms have been testing hundreds of land plants for biological activity. Following the logic of established bioactivity, a plant or animal that produces poisons, alkaloids, or other chemicals, may be the source of a medicinal drug that can kill cancer cells or microbes. The poppy provides such a prospect because a species of that plant is the source of opium and its component alkaloids, such as morphine. Poppies produce other—still untested—chemicals, and with their family connections, those compounds are well worth exploring.

The tactic of following in the footsteps of Chinese healers is gaining popularity with bioprospectors. Garcinone, derived

The opium poppy is the source of morphine and so is important in the treatment of pain. Other varieties of poppy have just recently come under study as possible sources of other medicines. (Courtesy of the Natural Resource Conservation Service)

The mangosteen tree was probably first cultivated in Thailand. The ripe fruit is round with a purplish skin. The rind is red, and the edible inner portion is white. The juice of the fruit is acclaimed as a refreshing drink; however, it is the rind that contains the chemicals that are likely to be of medical significance. (Courtesy of Jack Keller)

from the fruit of the mangosteen tree, has long been a part of traditional healing practices. This compound has shown the ability to help control liver cancer, a disease that has resisted most other chemical treatments.

Another possible source from traditional medicine comes from the flowering plant called wolf's bane. Known by many names, the one used by academic botanists is *Arnica montana*. The traditional use of flower extracts has been as a skin balm or muscle relaxant. If taken by mouth, the extract shows a tendency to cause rather than cure stomach cancer. However, this unfortunate effect has been caused by ingesting a crude extract. Researchers hope that an

This plant is variously known as leopard's bane or wolf's bane—and was sometimes used in an amulet to protect the wearer from wild animals. In traditional medicine, an extract was used as a skin balm. In this application, it is the source of arnica. Now, wider uses are being studied. (Courtesy of Project Runeberg, Scandinavia)

anticancer compound can be derived from the isolated and purified components of *Arnica montana*.

In sum, bioprospecting is a multifaceted undertaking with multiple goals and multiple strategies. The results could include marvelous cures for extremely dangerous diseases. The results could also include the enrichment of native people who have few other assets. Universities and pharmaceutical firms may also enjoy great monetary returns. However, when significant sums of money are involved, the weight of political influence will soon be experienced. Explorers and drug developers are well advised to proceed with some caution when laying claim to natural source materials.

Glossary

agonist   A substance that can interact with a receptor molecule and that initiates an action on the part of the receptor.

alkaloid   A family of carbon-based molecules that always include one or more nitrogen atoms. The typical alkaloid has a bitter taste. Caffeine and nicotine are common examples.

amino acid   A carbon-based molecule that contains nitrogen and is the building block for the assembly of proteins.

antagonist   A compound that opposes the action of another compound.

antibiotic   A compound that kills or stops the reproduction of microbes.

antibody   A protein produced by the immune system in response to exposure to a foreign molecule.

antigen   A compound that is foreign to the body and that induces the formation of antibodies.

antimicrobial   An agent that kills or inhibits the growth of microorganisms.

antispasmodic   A relaxant that will relieve or prevent involuntary contractions, as in muscle cramps.

archaeology   The study of the material remains of ancient societies.

artifact   An object produced by human craft.

Atabrine   The trade name for a synthetic compound similar to natural quinine.

bioprospecting   The search among biological organisms for commercially valuable compounds.

biosecurity The protection of people and natural resources from unwanted organisms capable of causing harm.

black bile Traditionally, the source of melancholy. Organically, the fluid produced by the gallbladder as an aid to the digestion of fats.

botulism An often fatal type of food poisoning caused by microbes.

cholera A severe and highly contagious infection of the intestinal system that is often fatal.

cultivar A cultivated variety of a domestic crop plant.

decoction A tea made of the bark and roots of a plant whereby these plant parts are simmered in boiling water.

diffusion The spread of ideas—as a metaphor based on the spread of a substance in a solution.

ecosystem An interacting collection of living and nonliving parts.

endocrine gland Organs that produce chemicals that are secreted directly into the bloodstream. The chemicals then control various bodily processes.

enzyme Protein-type molecules that direct the chemical reactions in biological cells.

epileptic seizure The acute stage of epilepsy characterized by jerky, convulsive movements and unconsciousness.

gasahol A mixture of about 90 percent gasoline and 10 percent ethyl alcohol used as fuel for automobiles.

glaucoma A condition of impaired vision due to hardening of the eyeball from internal pressure.

hallucinatory visions False perceptions that are often very dramatic but convincingly real.

harbinger An advance warning; an indicator of events to come.

herbal A document describing useful plants and often containing recipes for their use.

hormone A chemical that controls, guides, or activates a bodily process.

innovation   Changes in practices or in the design of products.

insulin   The hormone, produced by glands in the pancreas, that controls the use of sugar by body cells.

intellectual property   Generally, refers to inventions and copyrights but recently expanded to cover geographical factors such as the occupation of a particular territory and ownership of the biological resources therein.

interlocutor   A person who acts as a bridge or interpreter between two other persons; a translator.

invasive species   An animal pest or weed that can adversely affect indigenous species.

Jesuits   Members of a Roman Catholic order founded in 1534 noted for their discipline and scholarship.

lethality   The degree or extent of the ability to cause death.

marine environment   All areas in which the ocean and coast are significant parts—and all natural and biological resources contained therein.

medical physiologist   A biological scientist who specializes in studies of the bodily organs susceptible to disease.

metabolism   All the processes of building up and breaking down a biological substance; the chemical changes in a living cell.

mid-latitudes   The areas of the globe that lie between the Arctic Circle and the tropic of Cancer in the Northern Hemisphere and between the tropic of Capricorn and the Antarctic Circle in the Southern Hemisphere.

molecular biology   The study of biological processes at the molecular level with particular emphasis on the assembly of enzymes and other proteins.

moorland   A broad expanse of open land; often poorly drained and boggy.

morphine   An addictive alkaloid extracted from opium; used in medicine as a pain killer and sedative.

palliative   A compound that can reduce the symptoms of a disease but not cure it.

pharmacology   The study of medicinal materials; particularly their chemical composition, their application and their effects.

phlegm   Mucus.

placebo   An inactive substance administered as a comparison check in tests of the effectiveness of a drug.

poultice   A warm, moist mass of plant material applied to the skin either directly or over a cloth layer.

proprietary drug   A compound that has its name protected by a registered trademark and that can be dispensed without a doctor's prescription.

protein   A large, complicated carbon-based molecule with attached nitrogen that is a building block for all animal tissue.

proximity   Closeness.

puffer fish   A member of the family of fish that are able to swell in size when disturbed.

sauna   A steam bath originated in Finland that is generated by splashing water on heated rocks.

steroid   A carbon-based molecule that contains an alcohol attachment and is fat soluble. Steroids provide the basic molecule for the assembly of many hormones and vitamins.

sushi   Various dishes having raw fish as a primary ingredient.

sustainable use   The use of components of biological systems in a way and at a rate that does not lead to long-term decline in biological diversity.

therapeutic claims   The promises of medical effectiveness; often inflated for proprietary drugs.

tincture   Medicinal part of a plant extracted by an organic solvent such as alcohol, vinegar, or glycerin.

tonic   A drink that enhances a bodily function.

tranquilizer   A medical compound that reduces anxiety, calms, and relaxes the patient.

tuberculosis   A disease that can infect both humans and other animals. The symptoms include lesions of the lining of the lungs.

vedic medicine The medical materials and procedures developed within the Hindu culture of India.

yellow bile Choler, a product of the gallbladder needed for the digestion of fats.

yellow fever An infectious disease caused by a virus and characterized by jaundice or the development of a yellowish body color.

Further Reading

Balick, Michael, Elaine Elisabetsky, and Sarah Laird, eds. *Medicinal Resources of the Tropical Forest*. New York: Columbia University Press, 1995. An excellent introduction to the medicinal uses of tropical plants, including discussions on habitat protection and ethical issues in bioprospecting.

Barrett, S., and Gilda Knight. *The Health Robbers*. Philadelphia, Pa.: G. F. Stickley, 1993. Relates the ways in which dealers in patent medicines and nostrums have taken advantage of sick people who are desperate for relief.

Brechin, Steven, Peyer Wilshusen, Crystal Fortwangler, Patrick West, and Peter Wilshusen, eds. *Contested Nature: Promoting International Biodiversity and Social Justice in the Twenty-First Century*. Albany, N.Y.: SUNY Press, 2003. Contends that biological conservation and social justice must go hand in hand.

Crellin, John K., and Jane Philpott. *Herbal Medicine Past and Present*. Durham, N.C.: Duke University Press, 1989. This is a source book for studies of the people of rural America and their shared attitudes about health care.

Davis, Wade. *One River*. New York: Simon & Schuster, 1996. The author weaves back and forth between the story of his recent travels with the ethnobotanist Tim Plowman in the upper Amazon region and the key events in the South American expeditions carried out in the 1930s and 1940s by Richard Evans Schultes.

Forsyth, Adrian. *Tropical Nature: Life and Death in the Rainforests of Central and South America*. New York: Touchstone Books, 1987. A lively discussion of biodiversity and explanations of the ways in which species have adapted to the rainforest environment.

Friedman, David. *Focus on Drugs and the Brain.* Frederick, Md.: 21st Century Books, 1990. Takes a candid approach to the effects of various drugs. A readable and interesting discussion for young people.

Hubbell, Stephen. *The Unified Neutral Theory of Biodiversity and Biogeography.* Princeton, N.J.: Princeton University Press, 2001. Contains significant new ideas in ecology coupled with mathematical explanations.

Huntley, Beth. *Amazon Adventure.* Milwaukee, Wis.: Gareth Stevens, 1989. Colorfully illustrated virtual trip down the Amazon with attention to wildlife, plants, and native peoples.

Joyce, Christopher. *Earthly Goods.* Boston: Little, Brown, 1994. Covers the contributions of North and South American Indians to the assembly of useful medicines—with particular emphasis on curare and quinine.

Kaufman, Murray. *Reefs and Rain Forests: The Natural Heritage of Malaysian Borneo.* Kansas City, Kans.: Midpoint Trade Books, 2002. Beautifully illustrated description of one of the oldest natural habitats in the world.

Lerner, Carol. *Moonseed and Mistletoe: A Book of Poisonous Wild Plants.* New York: Morrow, 1988. Recommended as a reference source, it focuses on plants of North America.

Maxwell, Nicole. *Witch Doctor's Apprentice.* New York: Citadel Press, 1990. An autobiographical narrative that relates the author's adventures and dealings with other explorers, missionaries, and the native healers.

Peirce, Andrea. *The American Pharmaceutical Association Practical Guide to Natural Medicines.* New York: William Morrow, 1999. Covers the basic facts on over 200 herbs and nutritional supplements, including recommended dosages and information on effectiveness and safety.

Quinlan, Susan. *The Case of the Monkeys That Fell from the Trees: And Other Mysteries in Tropical Nature.* Honesdale, Pa.: Boyds Mills Press, 2003. Twelve ecological mysteries set in the tropical forests of Central and South America. Shows how the forests function.

Thomas, Peggy. *Medicines from Nature.* Washington, D.C.: 21st Century Books, 1997. A broad coverage of the adventures of ethnobotanists and their contributions to medicine.

Van Hagen, Victor W. *South America Called Them.* New York: Alfred A. Knopf, 1945. The adventures of La Condamine, Humboldt, and Spruce plus those of Charles Darwin.

Wagner, H., and Norman Farnswort, eds. *Economic and Medicinal Plant Research.* New York: Academic Press, 1991. Identifies the main directions of research from a practical point of view. Covers many topics, including antimalaria drugs and fungicides.

Web Sites

The following is a list of Web sites that provide up-to-date information about biomedical research, botanical studies, natural medicines and consumer issues. The list includes some of the most prominent academic and governmental organizations as well as some advocacy groups. The listings were valid as of February, 2005. If the address does not connect, try the organization's name or initials on your search engine. Also, just the search phrase "natural medicines" will bring up many relevant sites.

Academic Sites

Arizona Center for Phytomedicine Research. URL: http://acprx. pharmacy.arizona.edu. Accessed on March 4, 2005.

Fort Lewis College, Durango, Colorado, ethnobotany program. URL: http://anthro.fortlewis.edu/ethnobotany. Accessed on February 6, 2005.

Minnesota Institute for Sustainable Agriculture. URL: http://www. misa.umn.edu. Accessed on January 15, 2005.

Tulane University Program, Sociocultural Anthropology. URL: http://www.tulane.edu/~anthro/programs/socioinf.htm. Accessed on February 5, 2005.

University of Connecticut, program on Ecology and Evolutionary Biology. URL: http://hydrodictyon.eeb.uconn.edu/eebweb. Accessed on February 2, 2005.

University of Georgia, Laboratories of Ethnobiology. URL: http:// guallart.dac.uga.edu. Accessed on January 20, 2005.

University of Hawaii at Manoa ethnobotany program. URL: http://www.botany.hawaii.edu/ethnobotany. Accessed on January 25, 2005.

University of Kentucky, Natural Products Alliance. URL: http://www.ca.uky.edu/NPA. Accessed on February 16, 2005.

The University of Michigan at Dearborn Native American ethnobotany project. URL: http://herb.umd.umich.edu. Accessed on February 1, 2005.

University of Washington, Medicinal Herbal Garden. URL: http://nnlm.gov/pnr/uwmhg/walk.html. Accessed on February 5, 2005.

Government and International Agencies

Canadian Natural Health Products Directorate. URL: http://www.hc-sc.gc.ca/hpfb-dgpsa/nhpd-dpsn. Accessed on February 13, 2005.

National Institute of Arthritis and Musculoskeletal and Skin Diseases, Natural Products Section. URL: http://www.irp.niams.nih.gov/LabsBranches_groups.jsp?branchId=1&groupId=4. Accessed on February 5, 2005.

National Institutes of Health, National Center for Complementary and Alternative Medicine. URL: http://nccam.nih.gov. Accessed on February 3, 2005.

National Institutes of Health, Office of Dietary Supplements. URL: http://ods.od.nih.gov. Accessed on February 8, 2005.

Natural Products Branch, National Cancer Institute (Q&A). URL: http://cis.nci.nih.gov/fact/7_33.htm. Accessed on February 10, 2005.

U.S. Food and Drug Administration MedWatch program. URL: http://www.fda.gov/medwatch. Accessed on February 3, 2005.

Pharmaceutical Industry

Natural Products Industry Center (trade group). URL: http://www.npicenter.com. Accessed on February 10, 2005.

Natural Health and Longevity Resource Center (links to many information sources). URL: http://www.all-natural.com. Accessed on February 5, 2005.

Pharmaceutical Technology (trade group). URL: http://www. pharmaceutical-technology.com. Accessed on February 5, 2005.

Pharmaceutical Research and Manufacturers of America (PhRMA). URL: http://www.phrma.org. Accessed on February 10, 2005.

"Strategic Considerations for Screening Natural Products," by Dr. Matthew A. Sills. URL: http://www.netsci.org/Science/Screening/ feature10.html. Accessed on March 4, 2005.

Professional Societies

American Botanical Council. URL: http://www.herbalgram.org. Accessed on February 5, 2005.

American Herbalists Guild. URL: http://www.americanherbalist.com. Accessed on February 9, 2005.

National Institute of Medical Herbalists. URL: http://www.nimh.uk. Accessed on February 13, 2005.

Advocacy Groups

Alternative Medicine URL: http://hsl.mcmaster.ca/tomflem/alt med.html. Accessed on February 10, 2005.

American Heart Association (information on drug development). URL: http://www.americanheart.org/presenter.jhtml?identifier= 4700. Accessed on January 29, 2005.

Global Exchange (description of the relationship between bioprospecting and biopiracy). URL: http://www.globalexchange. org/countries/mexico/biopiracyReport.html. Accessed on February 9, 2005.

Pharmaceutical Nation. URL: http://www.pharmaceuticalnation.com. Accessed on February 10, 2005.

World Intellectual Property Organization. URL: http://www.wipo.int. Accessed on February 12, 2005.

General Interest

Bioprospecting describes an agreement between Colby College and the Merck Corporation to survey natural sources of medicines in Latin America. URL: http://www.colby.edu/personal/s/smshahve. Accessed on January 20, 2005.

The Brine Shrimp Project covers a science demonstration that can be conducted by students. URL: http://www.ncsu.edu/sciencejunction/terminal/lessons/brine.html. Accessed on December 27, 2004.

Plant Hunters outlines student field projects in botany. URL: http://pd.l2l.org/success/lessons/Lesson1/HSCa1_L.HTM. Accessed on February 7, 2005.

PlantExplorers.com describes the activities of a virtual botany club for people interested in plant photography and economic botany as a hobby. URL: http://www.plantexplorers.com. Accessed on February 7, 2005.

Patent Medicines page provides a brief historical view of the practices of self-medication and the related commercial developments. URL: http://www.cyberus.ca/~sjordan/pmhist.html. Accessed on February 10, 2005.

Index